Library of
Davidson College

Terranova

Terranova
The Ethos and Luck of Deep-Sea Fishermen

JOSEBA ZULAIKA

*A Publication of the
Institute for the Study of Human Issues
Philadelphia*

Copyright © 1981 by ISHI,
Institute for the Study of Human Issues, Inc.
All Rights Reserved
No part of this book may be reproduced in any form or by any electronic or mechanical means including information storage and retrieval systems without permission in writing from the publisher, except by a reviewer who may quote brief passages in a review.

Manufactured in the United States of America

Published in the United States by ISHI,
Institute for the Study of Human Issues, Inc.

Published in Canada by the
Institute of Social and Economic Research,
Memorial University of Newfoundland,
as No. 25 in the series *Social and Economic Studies*

Library of Congress Cataloging in Publication Data

Zulaika, Joseba.
　Terranova: the ethos and luck of deep-sea fishermen.

　　Bibliography: p.
　　Includes index.
　　1. Fisheries—Spain—Sociological aspects. 2. Fishermen—Spain—Socioeconomic status. 3. Fishermen—Spain—Psychology. 4. Cod-fisheries—Grand Banks of Newfoundland. 5. Trawls and trawling—Spain. I. Title.
SH285.Z84　　306'.3　　80-20931
ISBN 0-89727-016-9

For information, write:

Director of Publications
ISHI
3401 Science Center
Philadelphia, Pennsylvania 19104
U.S.A.

Contents

Acknowledgements vi
Figures and Photographs vii
Preface ix

1. The *Pareja* as a Social Institution 1
   The Organization of the Pareja 1
   Spatial and Social Structures on Board 16

2. Near and Distant Relations 33
   Returning Home 34
   Foreign Harbour 42
   Shipboard Social Relations 45
   Epilogue: "Being a Fisherman" 56

3. The Order of Luck 65
   The Problem of Chance 65
   Fishermen's Conception of Luck 68
   Luck on Our Voyage 69
   The Ambivalence of Luck 75
   Luck and the Daily Catch 77
   Luck and the Ritual of Fishing 81
   The Pesca and the Ritual of Fishing 82
   Luck and Fatalism among Fishermen 87
   Disorder: A Sign of Luck 90

4. "Terranova Is a Very Round Wheel" 95

Appendix: Fluctuations of Catches 109
References 116
Index 119

Acknowledgements

This monograph is a revised version of an M.A. thesis submitted to the Department of Anthropology of Memorial University. I am indebted to my supervisor, Frank Manning, for his help with the general organization of the thesis; and to Raoul Andersen, Rex Clark, Geoffrey Stiles, Adrian Tanner, and especially Jean Briggs, who read parts of the first draft and provided substantial comments and elucidations on basic points. I got many new ideas from long conversations with Judy Adler. Father J. Beobide offered valuable information and criticism, and supplied the photographs that are credited to him. The staff of the Spanish Seamen's Centre in St. John's helped me in many ways.

The Newfoundland writer Percy Janes patiently went over the first draft making corrections in English grammar and spelling. The present version owes an enormous amount to Sonia Kuryliw Paine's extensive editing and re-writing. I am most grateful to her. Special thanks are also due to Robert Paine, who encouraged me to convert the thesis into a book and undertook the final editorial responsibility. Jeanette Gleeson wended her way through the many corrections to bring it all together in a cleanly typed manuscript.

My greatest gratitude is to the fishermen themselves: Luciano, Vicente, Poldo, Agustín, Manolo, Felix, Ramiro, Julio, Manolo, Lustres, Parada, Ramiro, Francisco, Jesús, Leopoldo, Moncho, José, Manuel, Paco, Manolo, Valentín, Gonzalo, Pancho, Antonio, and Juan. They gave me their friendship, and I hope they will not be displeased with this work whose aim is to make known their waning occupation and way of life.

The Institute of Social and Economic Research, Memorial University, financed the field work.

The Canadian edition of this book has been published with the help of a grant from the Social Science Federation of Canada, using funds provided by the Social Sciences and Humanities Research Council of Canada.

Figures and Photographs

Figures

1. Lines of recruitment in a *pareja*   8
2. The authority structure as delegated by the shipowner   9
3. The formal authority structure of the *pareja*   10
4. The ship's layout   18-19
5. The structural position of the three petty officers   24

Photographs

PHOTOGRAPHS FOLLOW PAGE 64.

The *pareja* in harbour
Splicing broken cables
The full net rises to the surface
A view of the cables from deck
Hauling in the net
Fishermen emptying the net
Processing fish on board
A trawler's engine room
A salter at work
Some difficulties of work on a trawler
Singing with a flourish
Expressive boozing

Preface

This study is concerned with the approximately 2,000 Spanish deep-sea fishermen whose livelihood has traditionally been the catching of codfish in the North Atlantic seas. "Terranova," although it literally refers only to Newfoundland, is the Spanish name that for centuries has lumped together the Northwest Atlantic waters; in the Northeast Atlantic are the Norwegian fishing grounds, visited only recently by Spanish seamen.

Rather than add more data to the technological or economic aspects of deep-sea fishing, my search has been for its "sociocultural concomitants" that thus far "are only fragmentarily and unsystematically documented" (Andersen and Wadel 1972: 164). More specifically, my concern is with *fishing as a cultural system* (cf. Geertz 1973), and my aim is to uncover the modes of thought developed by the fishermen in the course of pursuing their occupation. Natural, social and conceptual facts, and how they are ordered at sea in creating a certain cultural context, are explored; as such the focus of this analysis can be viewed as being primarily on the relations between man and nature as they become translated into social, emotional and ideational categories. This perspective has the advantage of partially avoiding the question of how far the "fishing culture" of the Spanish Terranova fishermen is simply a common Spanish culture carried to the sea from land. Some of the issues that fishermen's natural and mental ecology brings forth can be stated as: how men conceptually order their environment;

how economic needs legitimize institutional deprivation; how distance shapes emotional relations.

Fishermen's behaviour points out the limitations of a theory that describes their social life basically in terms of the ship's physical and psychological isolation (Aubert 1965: 236-58). Although granting full validity to the total institutional features of the ship, this volume claims that fishing generates its own cultural context (the institutional aspect being one fundamental aspect of it) and that without particular attention to this context, any analysis of the fishing occupation remains incomplete.

Despite my initial expectations that the social-structural or institutional elements among deep-sea fishermen would be the main ethnographic area of description, I soon realized that the formal social organization, as such, was secondary in the cultural context aboard ship. Since "luck" and longing to "return" (home) were the factors that really seemed to determine the everyday experience, cognitive and affective relations appeared central to any cultural analysis of the Terranova fishing occupation.

It could well be argued that these relations are ultimately the result of socio-economic circumstances and that change in these circumstances would automatically change their cultural manifestations. For instance, one might contend that a secure wage would free the fishermen from dependence on luck. Although there is much to this argument, what we are interested in here are those cultural "symptoms" that point to larger issues. It is not simply that the expression of cognitive and affective culture forms an indissoluble system with the socio-economic structure; it is also that the permanency of the structure is significantly maintained by the other elements of the cultural system.

Technologically, Spanish fishing in Terranova is carried out by two different means: the *bou* and the *pareja*. The *bou* is a single large trawler, whereas the *pareja*, or "pair," consists of two trawlers dragging jointly, each of the trawl's two wings being pulled by a trawler. The present ethnography deals with the social unit formed by the twenty-six men in each of two trawlers in the *pareja* system.

The field work was carried out during a complete fishing

voyage, which began in the home port of Vigo (on the northwest coast of Spain) on 21 August 1976 and ended on 9 January 1977. After ten days, the *pareja* reached the Greenland Banks, where the trawlers fished for twenty days until an engine problem forced a trip to St. John's. For the rest of the voyage, the *pareja* fished off the Newfoundland coast, mainly on the Grand Banks, Bank of St. Pierre, and Banquereau.

In the past, Terranova fishermen have made two or even three voyages per year, and in recent years each voyage yielded about a thousand tons of processed fish. However, in January, 1977, because of declining fish stocks, Canada imposed a quota of 300 tons of processed fish per year on foreign ships operating within the new 200-mile limit (Warner 1977). (In 1978 the quota was reduced to 150 tons.) A single voyage is now more than sufficient to catch the maximum tonnage of fish. The obvious consequence of this sudden reduction of the catches to about one-seventh of the potential is practically the end of Spanish fishing in the North Atlantic. This ethnography is not, however, intended as a description of a vanishing 'traditional' fishing culture. Although the particular cultural *context* described here is likely to disappear, the cultural *systemic elements* that deep-sea fishing, as an industrial adaptation, presents should be applicable to other fishing crews in similar conditions.

I participated in the voyage as a full crew member in the role of cookee (assistant to the cook). Because Galician labour is cheap, the shipowner would accept only Galician deckhands, and therefore I was grateful to the cook (who was Basque like myself) for his willingness to take me, this being the only possible way I could join a *pareja*. Although I kept my purpose secret at the beginning of the voyage for fear of being isolated by the crew, as soon as I made friends with them I revealed my intentions; there was no negative reaction. My relations with the entire crew (including the officers) were excellent during the whole voyage, with the exception of some minor incidents. The role of cookee happened to be ideal for my field work because, more than any other job, it put me in constant interaction with all the groups on board. Moreover, the position of cookee is considered the lowest.

Even the fishermen regard the cookee as an inferior; any service can be demanded of him, and he frequently serves as the butt of jokes. This position gave me some unusual insights into the social structure that I might not have gained otherwise.

CHAPTER 1

The Pareja as a Social Institution

The *pareja* system of fishing (a "pair" of cod-trawlers dragging conjointly) has been in operation only since the 1940s. Previously, the *bou* was used to fish the Terranova waters.[1] In 1976, the proportion of *bous* to *parejas* was 10 (with an average crew of 45) to 34 (with an average crew of 50). Many *pareja* fishermen have had previous experience working on *bous*.

This introductory chapter outlines the basic features of the *pareja*: the technological, economic and legal aspects that give this fishery its particular structure, as well as its division of power. The two trawlers of the *pareja* make up one economic and operational unit under the same power structure; however, each of the two crews constitutes a separate social unit.

The Organization of the Pareja

TECHNOLOGY

No fishing operation can be carried out by one trawler in a *pareja*. Each trawler has its own trawl (net) composed of two wings moored to a winch. For the dragging, one wing of the trawl is moored to the starboard side of one trawler's winch (the trawler whose net is dragging is always placed on the starboard side), and the other wing is given to the companion trawler (or sister ship), which fixes it on the portside of its winch. When trawler A hauls in the net, after receiving the wing that trawler B seizes through the cord attached to it from inside the net, then it is trawler B's turn to "shoot away" (lower) its own net, while trawler A stores the fish caught and seizes the portside wing of B's trawl.

In our *pareja* two casts, each of about ten hours' duration, were done per day, or alternatively three casts of seven hours each. One lance ("throw") means two different manoeuvres: *largar* (to let the net out) and *virar* (to haul the net in), which together take about one and a half hours to complete, depending on the volume of the catch. A day of two casts means that both trawlers come together four times for the operation of taking or giving a wing of the trawl.

The net is the constant bond, bringing together both trawlers for a single purpose. Sometimes the manoeuvres of hauling in the net of one's own trawler and letting out the companion's net are done at once; at other times, depending on the yield of the area, distance is covered between the two manoeuvres in order to get to other places or to go back to repeat the same dragging. The turn of the trawlers in the throw was strictly observed during our whole voyage.

Each trawler is equipped with modern gear which, in our *pareja*, included two fish finders to detect the fish, two echo-sounders, Decca radar RR 914, Decca radar RM 316, loran, gyroscopic rudder, manual rudder, UHF radiophonic system. Panasonic 23-channel citizen-band transceiver.

In the fishing technology of the *pareja*, the composition of the trawl occupies an outstanding place. Each *pesca* (technician in charge of strategy; see below) makes up his own trawl in a different way, according to his own experience and expertise, the success of which gives him his reputation. The trawl is a complicated construction of nets (the main parts of which are usually known as wings, bellies and cod end), bobbins (heavy steel roller balls that keep the net dragging on the bank), floats (aluminum balls that lift the net vertically), and towing hawsers of different diameters. The weight of each trawl amounts to approximately seven tons.

The Pareja as a Social Institution

During the two manouevres of letting out and hauling in the net, the crew positions are the following: On the bridge, the *pesca* supervises from the central window that opens on the deck; the helmsman, under his orders, keeps the trawler in position. On deck, the boatswain, the foreman responsible for the fishermen's technical performance, and the single connection between deck and bridge, holds the attention of all the fishermen; three winchmen (and two deckhands during the hauling in) are on the winch in the forward part of the deck; the remaining eleven or nine deckhands are strategically distributed on each side of the deck. The engineer on duty is ready to carry out the *pesca's* orders, received through a telephone that connects with the bridge, regarding the engine and winch power to be used. The synchronization of the eighteen men requires total attention during the manoeuvres.

Once the two trawlers have come together, the manoeuvre of letting the net out starts. The cod end is hauled in to the stern side with a snatch block and let out while the trawler is moving ahead. (Each time that work with the net is held up in its run across the deck, or that ropes, bridles, wing rubbers, floats and bobbins are entangled, the deckhands jump over, clear up the problem, and return to their positions.) The wing-end bobbins are stuck with stoppers at each side of the deck. The portside wing-end bobbin is coupled with a rope. A heaving line is thrown over to the companion trawler, and this line is moored to the rope that is coupled with the starboard wing-end bobbin, which will go to the companion trawler's winch. The stoppers connecting the trawl at the ramp are let go and the wing-end bobbins pass out through the ramp. The hawser is loosened according to the depth of the water and then coupled in the tow-rope hook.

The manoeuvre of hauling in is still more complex. With the two trawlers side by side, the hawsers are taken into the winch, until the portside wing-end bobbin reaches the ramp. A rope, which goes inside the net and ties together both wing-end bobbins of the trawl, is moored to a hawser that takes in the starboard wing-end bobbin, previously attached to the companion trawler. Once both wing-end bobbins are in the performing trawler's ramp, they are hooked to hawsers that haul them back to the winch, where they are fixed. The heavy hooks coming from the bridge tower are taken back and fastened to the straps encircling each wing of the trawl, and hauled in again and again, until the bobbins appear. If the haul is big, double and triple blocks are needed to take in the cod end. When the cod end is on the deck, the rope knot that ties the tail is let go and the fish tumble into the park through the hatches. Sometimes even the triple block cannot take in the whole net, and the operation called *saquear* is necessary. It consists of making use of a metallic belly-line that goes around the net and pulls back the terminal part of the cod end, which is then taken in six tons at a time until the whole cod end can be hauled in.

The second and more tedious part of fishermen's work is fish-processing, which in a *pareja* can easily take fifteen to twenty hours. This includes five steps: selection of the fish (good cod is "clean" and small cod or any other species is "garbage" to be thrown to the sea, a practice being eliminated now by a few companies whose ships have been provided with cold-storage); heading, which in our trawler was performed both manually and mechanically; splitting, performed manually and with two splitting machines; mechanized cleaning; manual salting and storage.

At times, the net comes in broken and four, six or all the fishermen spend long hours repairing it. This activity, carried out on deck with bare hands during the freezing days and nights of a Terranova winter, causes the fishermen memorably cruel hours. Knowledge of the net and efficiency in repairing it are regarded as core skills.

ECONOMICS

A question that brings us directly to the nature of the fishing institution of the *pareja* is: How does the *pareja* serve the ends of (1) the shipowner, (2) the officers, and (3) the fishermen?

The Spanish fleet that fishes in Terranova is privately owned. In 1976 it comprised ten *bous*, owned by a shipping company; the rest of the fleet, an estimated thirty-four *parejas*, was in the hands of individual owners. For the owner, the *pareja* means an invest-

The Pareja as a Social Institution

ment of about 200 million pesetas ($3 million), and his aim is to earn a profit comparable to that in other industries. It is interesting to note the increase in shipbuilding in Spain recently. At the beginning of the 1960s the Spanish government had a choice of alternative developments for the fishing industry. The first was to increase the exploitation of coastal resources, which implied a large financial outlay for the expansion of harbour facilities and for a bio-ecologic investigation of the continental platform to determine the optimum fishing possibilities; the second was the creation of a modern deep-sea fleet with a capitalist mode of production, implying more investment for the construction of large trawlers, with the latest in new technology. The government chose the second alternative, and the massive shipbuilding program offered entrepreneurs loans of up to 83 percent of the total cost of production. In addition, incentive bonuses and tax reductions were used as a stimulus for ship construction. The rejected policy was supportive of inshore fishing, whereas the one adopted proved extremely detrimental to the inshore fishery.

The total income of our voyage in 1977, according to the report of the shipowner who privately sets the sale price on an unfixed basis with the retail outlet, was almost $1 million, distributed as follows: 48 percent went to salaries, and between 16 and 25 percent to preparation and maintenance. When asked about the shipowner's net profit, the officers' estimate was between 20 and 30 percent, but the shipowner himself dismissed this figure as unrealistically high.

The wages were calculated on the basis of a percentage of the gross profits, plus a minimal wage of 6,700 pesetas (about $100) per month. At the end of the voyage, this minimum—which was roughly the same for officers and fishermen—amounted to 10 percent of the fishermen's final wage; therefore seamen dismiss this minimal figure as irrelevant and regard the percentage of the catch as the actual salary. A clause in our contract also guaranteed a wage of 20,537.50 pesetas (about $300) per month, in case the sum of the minimal wage plus our share of the catch did not reach the guaranteed figure. However, in our contracts there was no time limit on the length of the voyage; this, translated into economic terms, meant that since ideally we were going to fill up the holds, the monthly wage was to be calculated by dividing the gross profit by the number of months spent at sea.[2] To fill up the holds in three months or in six months meant that in the first case we were going to earn roughly twice as much as in the second. The contract did allow for a stipend of 25,000 pesetas (about $360) in case we had to stay at sea during Christmas.

The salaries of the *pesca*, captain, chief engineer, and to a lesser extent, the remaining four engineers were very good in terms of percentages.[3] The fishermen also earned good wages; according to the profits made on our voyage, the wages on a coastal fishing boat or on a merchant ship were half and three-quarters, respectively, of the amount earned in a *pareja*.

The percentage salaries on our *pareja* were as follows: first *pesca*, 6 percent;[4] second *pesca*, 1.5; captain of the first trawler, 1.5; chief engineer of the first trawler, 1.25; captain of the second trawler, 1; chief engineer of the second trawler, 1; second engineers, 0.75; third engineers, boatswains and chief salters, 0.5; cooks, 0.45; twenty-five fishermen, two helmsmen, six oilers, and two cookees, 0.35. The top man on the scale earned four times as much as the second on the scale and eighteen times as much as the men at the bottom. In addition to the percentage wage there was the relatively small basic wage (the captain's being somewhat larger than the *pesca*'s).

One advantage that the fishermen emphasize about working in Terranova is the "compulsory" saving. At home their earnings would be spent in socializing; on a merchant ship they would be in port frequently and therefore spending money; at Terranova they work almost the entire voyage and cannot spend their money until they arrive home.

AUTHORITY STRUCTURE

Within the internal order of the ship there is a double structure of authority—one headed by the *pesca* and the other by the captain. The interplay between these two structures and how the shipowner puts it to use is an important aspect of the institutional reality of the *pareja*. The pattern of recruitment flows from the shipowner. He personally chooses a *pesca* to whom he "gives" the *pareja* in the sense that the *pesca* is the only person responsible to him. As to the captain's appointment, the general opinion among *pareja* fishermen is that the captain is personally chosen by the *pesca*. In order to get the *pareja* ready for sailing, the shipowner selects an inspector, who is usually responsible for finding the chief engineers and the personnel for the engine rooms. The remainder of the crew is recruited as shown in Figure 1.

The saying goes that "the shipowner[5] gives the *pareja* to the *pesca*." He is the communicating link with the owner regarding major decisions, such as when to begin or end the voyage, the extension or reduction of the time at sea, unexpected visits to harbour, the volume of supplies on board, and repairs to be made in harbour; moreover, all decision-making regarding fishing strategy, location, schedules, and other such matters is in the hands of the *pesca* as he alone is responsible for the success of the voyage. Therefore, his authority at sea is supreme over both trawlers.

What makes one trawler first and the other second (en route the first always goes ahead) is the location of the first *pesca*. (In this volume, all references to *pesca* mean first *pesca*.) The second *pesca*'s authority is reduced to directing the technical manoeuvres of the second trawler, in close contact with first *pesca*'s orders. Thus, any decision regarding a fishing operation affects both trawlers equally. Similarly, the captain of the first trawler is responsible for the captain of the second trawler (however, we shall see later that this hierarchy is very unstable). Each captain has formal jurisdiction over his own ship, and as such he is also in direct communication with the shipowner regarding matters that concern safety guarantees and the crew's contractual relations; nevertheless, the second trawler depends on the first trawler's decisions concerning a fishing operation. A radio system connecting both trawlers' bridges is thus essential to efficient decision-making.[6]

How do the two structures of authority (the one delegated

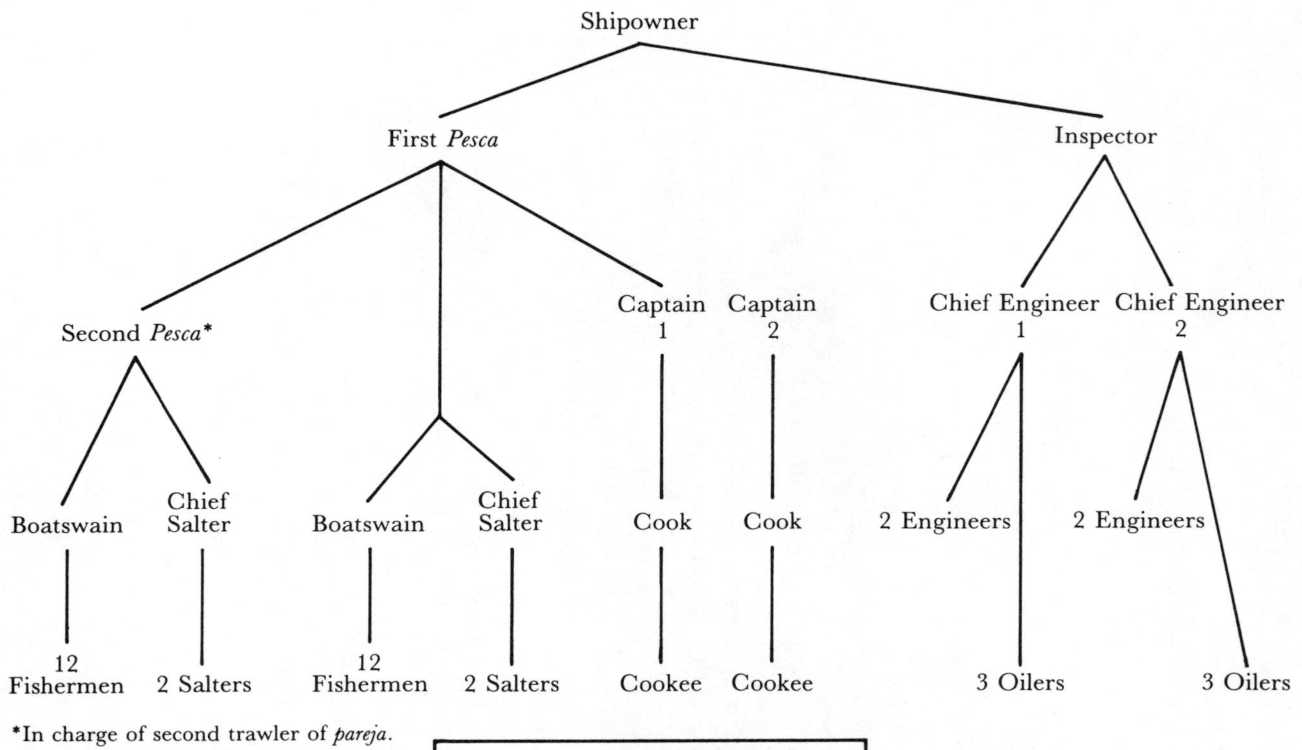

FIGURE 1

Lines of Recruitment in a Pareja

*In charge of second trawler of *pareja*.

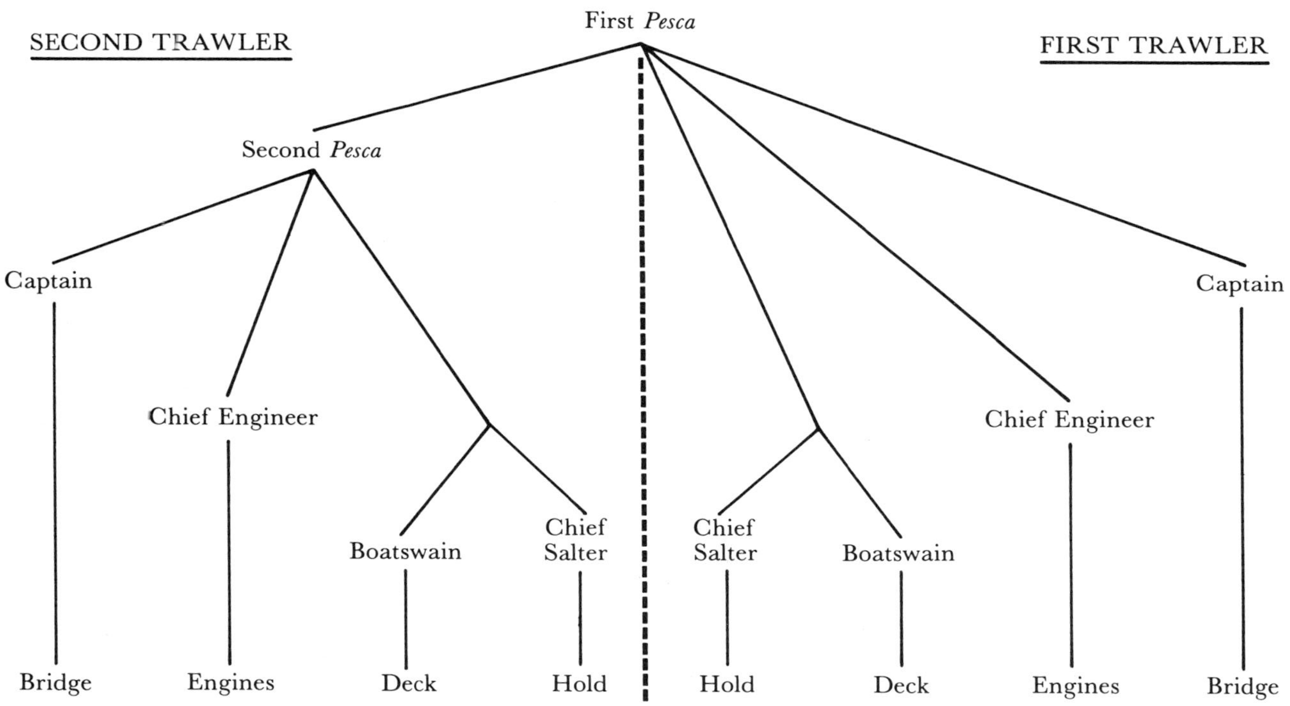

FIGURE 2

The Authority Structure as Delegated by the Shipowner

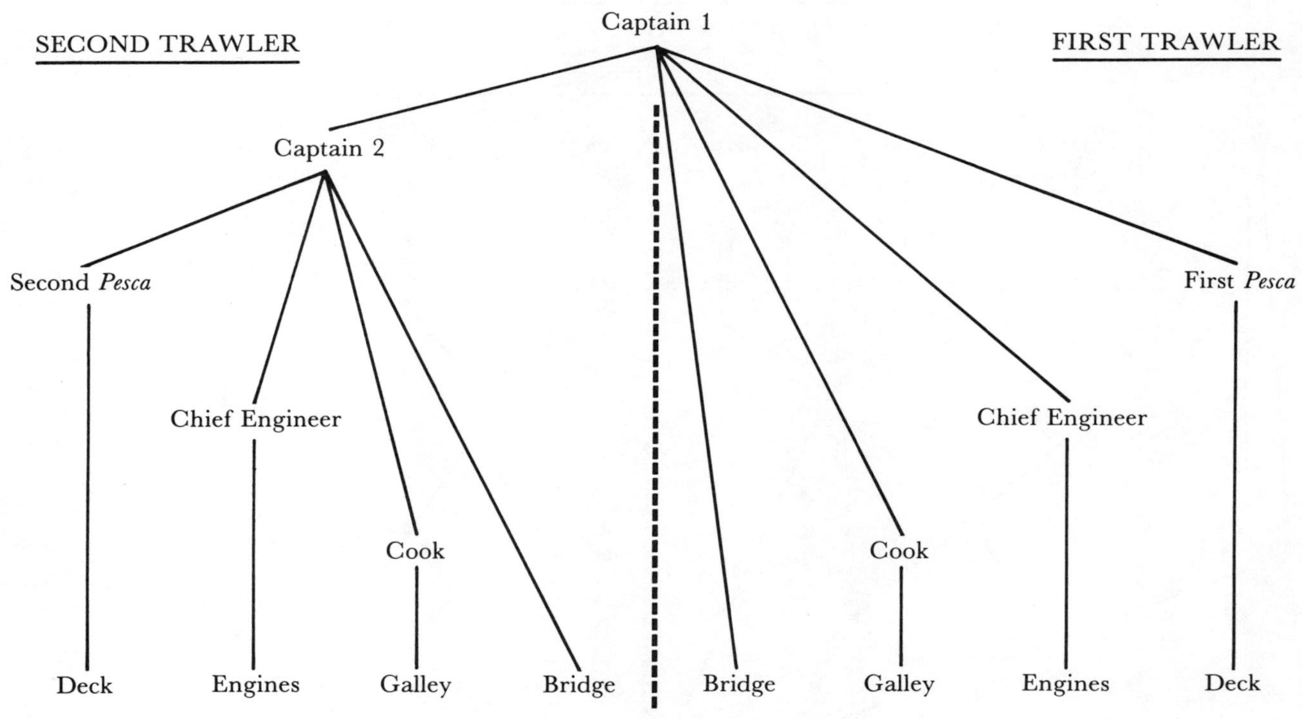

FIGURE 3

The Formal Authority Structure of the Pareja

from the entrepreneur, the other arising from the institutional structure)—see Figures 2 and 3—coexist in a *pareja*? On my first visit to a *pareja* in St. John's harbour, I was told (to my surprise) that the captain, although he holds the maximum authority, does not command on board. "At sea the one who commands is the *pesca*; in harbour it is the captain," was the clearest explanation. In other words, all fishing strategy is ordered by the *pesca*, whereas judicial matters belong to the captain. The *pesca* himself once replied to the cook's protests over his being late for lunch, in harbour, in this way: "I am one more fisherman in port; tell the captain what you have to say"; that is, in harbour the formal institutional authority takes over. Another way fishermen explain the distribution of authority between the *pesca* and the captain is: "In everything that concerns fishing, the *pesca* gives the orders; all the captain does is take the ship where the *pesca* orders him to take it."

It is obvious that the *pesca* holds the real power on board, and the captain's subordination is made quite clear by the fact that his appointment depends on the *pesca*'s discretion. (Our *pesca*, for example, had changed captains twice in the two previous years). For the crew in general, the captain's authority is on a formal level, and since it is the captain who is responsible for everyday administration and discipline, the captain's role also protects the *pesca*'s role.

Costa is the name given to the officer with the title "Patron of Deep-Sea Fishing Official," whose main task is to take the ship to the point where the *pesca* has ordered him. Contrary to the sovereignty that a captain enjoys on his ship, including the *pesca*'s submission to his juridical control, a *costa* is an official who fulfills the same navigational functions as the captain but without his formal authority; in the absence of a captain, however, this changes. For example, in St. John's harbour, I visited several *parejas* whose power pyramid consisted of two *pescas* and two *costas*, in which case either the *pesca* or the *costa* figures as captain for juridical purposes.

In our *pareja* the first trawler had a captain who figured as captain (not as *costa*), whereas the second trawler had a captain who figured as *costa* (so I was told) for the Spanish marine authorities. In general, the *pesca*-captain relationship at sea was understood by the crew in the traditional line of *pesca-costa*, in which the *pesca* is responsible for fishing strategy and the shipowner's interests, and the *costa* strictly for nautical knowledge (under orders from the *pesca*).[7]

THE LAW AND THE PAREJA

Juridically, life aboard a Spanish ship is under the Penal and Disciplinary Law, which can be considered "almost military rule" (Soroa 1976a). The substantive penal legislation, as well as the assignment of any offence to the Marine Military Jurisdiction, ensures that, ultimately, any infraction on board can be dealt with by military law. Thus, strictly speaking, life on board a fishing or merchant vessel is under "permanent militarization."

A practical example of this militarization is the term used to describe the refusal to work; instead of "strike," it is "sedition" (art. 24-a of the LPDMM[8] of 1955). An act of 'sedition' occurred in a *bou* trawler during the fall of 1976. According to article 106, five months is the maximum period of time at sea, but this can be extended to seven "for justified reasons of fishing exploitation." After five months, the crew of the *bou* decided, against the shipowner's will, to go home and refused to work. Their action was considered seditious, and the instigator of the strike agreed with the captain to take responsibility for it alone instead of implicating the whole crew. At the time the captain of the seditious trawler reported the incident to me, the instigator was waiting to be put in jail.

Similarly, leaving a trawler without permission is "desertion" (art. 45 of the LPDMM). The fishermen reminded me of a recent case in St. John's harbour which, although rare, is appropriate to relate here. As a result of a conflict between the *pesca* and the captain, the *pesca* abandoned the ship; opposing the shipowner's order to stay at sea, the fishermen, in support of the *pesca*, left their trawler and joined the companion trawler's crew to return to Spain. They were considered guilty of desertion and were

The Pareja as a Social Institution

punished by the shipowner, who did not pay them at all for the voyage. An example of the shipowner's exploitation of the crew's lack of legal protection is the insulting letter he wrote to the fishermen's wives, stating that "in case he [the husband-fisherman] does not finish the voyage, we will deduct money from the wage of his new job."

Rigid discipline, a strict hierarchy, elitism, and work considered as a "service" to be sanctioned by reward or punishment dominate the whole Ordinance of Work that regulates life on board. The lengthy section XIV, which deals with "Rewards, Faults and Sanctions," is particularly revealing. The following belong to the "very grave faults" for any of which the punishment can be "suspension of work and salary from three to five months" or "dismissal with total loss of rights": "drunkenness in an act of service, habitual blasphemy, voluntary and continued diminution of the normal output of work, simulation of illness and accident" (art. 132). Although our officers never made use of it, the power of this law was available.

The fishermen's juridical impotence makes it likely that any arbitrary order will make them think of getting justice in terms of personal vengeance. This was the case on our trawler when the chief engineer forced two engineers and three oilers to work a daily schedule of twelve hours, when eight is the number stipulated in normal conditions. All they could do to contain their anger was to plot vengeance when the voyage was over, and to avoid working with this man another time.

However, the *pareja* seamen like to praise their situation after comparing it with the militarization of the *bou* system. In general, it is said that the *bous* are "more dictatorial" and the *parejas* "more democratic." The reality is that the *parejas* and the *bous* are ultimately under the same penal law, subject to military jurisdiction. But the crewmen in the *parejas* are duped, through the democracy of their social relations, into thinking that they are better off than their comrades under the military-like social organization of the *bous*, where a turn of six hours of work is followed by another turn of six hours of rest. In a *pareja* no schedule, no night, no holiday, no time of rest is observed at all, and the crew could potentially be forced to work a twenty-four-hour shift. The 'modernization' of the social relations on board the *pareja*, in the sense of there being closer relations between officers and fishermen, is used to cover up the deterioration of working conditions. However, the *pareja* seamen are aware of the exploitative developments that have taken place in the last three to five years. Since 1973, the traditional Christmas break at home, lasting until the final days of January, has not been in effect because the recent shortage of fish necessitates lengthening the period at sea so that the trawlers can return home with their holds filled up. In the same year the *pareja* crews started working day and night. At first they were paid for each night of work; soon night work became part of the unwritten schedule, and today it has to be taken for granted by anybody joining a *pareja*. The *pesca* takes full advantage of the lack of a schedule, which constitutes the hardest working condition in a *pareja*.

In terms of catches the difference between the two systems of fishing is enormous. The actual earnings in a *pareja* are about one-third more than in a *bou*. Economic advantages and the democratic milieu are the *pareja*'s compensation for the exploitation of the seamen's contracts.

The peculiar militarization of the Spanish fishing industry has been facilitated by the absence of seamen's trade unions. (Unions were outlawed during Franco's regime.) A good example of this lack of union protection is the kind of contract our crew was offered; we were asked to sign blank forms, trusting the verbal promises of the shipowner. We all knew that refusal to sign could mean no job, for it was easy for him to get workers among the many unemployed fishermen. The percentage figures that actually appeared on the contracts later were substantially lower than those verbally promised (0.22 percent as compared to 0.35 percent).

Tight control is exercised by shipowners with regard to outside interference.[9] Two priests who embarked on the Terranova fleet in the late 1960s provoked the shipowners' strong oppostion. When the priests attempted to expose the fishermen's unjust working conditions, the shipowners denounced the effort as "nonconstructive social propaganda"; the owners even pressured the

French administration, through the Chamber of Commerce, to forbid the Spanish priests and the "Stella Maris" organization to remain in the French territory of St. Pierre by threatening to stop the Spanish fleet from docking in the port.[10]

The official body that is set up to protect the legal rights of seamen is a military organization divided into Comandancia de Marina ("Marine Command") and Ayudantia de Marina ("Marine Adjutancy"), both headed by military men. On our own voyage we had an opportunity to test the effectiveness of the Marine Command. The day before leaving home port, we went out to sea for a trial run and did not return until 1 A.M.; as no other transportation was available, a group of fishermen who lived nearby asked the shipowner for a taxi to take them home (a legal right according to the Ordinance's art. 100). The shipowner's rejection of the fishermen's request (it would have cost him about $75) provoked a row which ended in the expulsion of eight fishermen from the *pareja*; and, what was more important, the commander marked on their *cartilla* (book of employment) a 'stain' that could hinder their future employment as fishermen. The Marine Command did not come to their aid.

A fact that contributes to this militarization is that a ship is considered part of the national territory—with a peculiar physical mobility.[11] On the whole, what Soroa (1976b: 1) points out regarding the merchant marine is applicable to the fishing fleet as well: "In fact, it is known by everybody that court-martial for sedition, desertion, insult to a superior, or any other 'great' offences typified in the LPDMM has rarely been applied as an actual weapon against the claims or struggles of the merchant marine. Normally, the mere possibility of court-martial (the intimidating effect) has been sufficient, combined with the accumulation of little administrative threats from the Marine Command and Adjutancies (for example, noting in the *cartilla* the reasons for travelling; the powers of the commander over any maritime enrollment; and the merchant sailor's ignorance of his rights and his juridical condition)."[12]

Finally, it need hardly be stressed that the maintenance of the paramilitary legal status of the ship is in the interest of the Spanish shipowners, who are safely able to amortize their loans by the availability of a cheap and highly controlled labour force.

Spatial and Social Structures on Board

SPATIAL ORGANIZATION OF THE TRAWLER

The singular importance of the spatial distribution on board ship became obvious to me from the very first day at the home port of Vigo. Jumping from the wharf to the deck, I followed the cook, who in search of the galley went directly down to the lower deck, which is divided into four compartments. From stern to bow, first came the engine-room; next, connected with the stern side of the deck by a fishtrap, was the "park," the department where the fish is processed; then came the fishermen's mess and cabins, where their leisure life takes place; and forward were the stores and refrigerators to hold the food supplies. (See Figure 4.) But there was no galley. Two hatches, one at the food store and another at the park, gave access to the deck below, which, apart from the space occupied by the machinery, was mostly taken up by the hold, where the salted fish was stored. "This seems to be a ship without a galley," growled the cook.

Back on the main deck, we climbed the steps to the bridge deck. From portside to starboard, at the bow side of the corridor, were the cabins of the chief engineer, engineers (a double), *pesca* and captain. At the stern side were steps descending to the main deck and the cabins below, steps to the upper bridge (where all the fishing and navigation instruments were placed), the officers' washroom, the officers' mess, and a small room called "office," from which the meals were served and where the dishes were washed. This office had a lift that communicated with the galley.

The bridge stood centred above the main deck. On the portside of the bridge, at the deck level, was the gangway to the fishermen's cabins and washrooms; on the starboard side we finally found the galley. At the sharp bow of the deck was the net-supplies store, behind which lay the winch; from the winch to the ramp the deck lay open to the sea.[13]

The Pareja as a Social Institution

The spatial layout of the ship had a significant influence on the social structure of the crew. The overall division was between up and down, that is, between bridge and deck, officers and fishermen; the captain, the *pesca*, and the three engineers were up, whereas the three petty-officers (boatswain, chief salter and cook), helmsman (although his working territory was on the bridge), thirteen fishermen, three oilers, and cookee were down.

The deck, the fishermen's working space, included the following places: the upper or main deck where the fishing operations were carried out, the park where the fish was processed, and the hold where the fish was salted and stored. According to each stage of the work, "deck" meant "the place of the manoeuvre," and "park-hold" where the fish was processed. In the second stage of fish-processing, "deck" was used to mean "park" to differentiate the "park" from the "hold." On days when there was a big catch, I was expected to help the fishermen, and their question, while I was putting on the long rubber boots, was: "Where are you going, to the deck [park] or to the hold?" On other occasions, "up" would be substituted for deck and "down" for hold.

The up or down status was spatially indicated by two separate messes, one on the bridge for the 'uppers' (officers and engineers), the other on the lower deck for the rest. There was no significant difference in the quality of the food for each group. Particularly during meals, both groups referred frequently to the space of the other group as "up" or "down." The galley was between up and down; my role as cookee, and to a lesser degree the cook's role, was to communicate with both territories and take frequent messages "up" and "down."

Sleeping quarters are also spatially segregated along the same status lines. Officers and engineers retire to the between-deck area on the bridge, whereas the fishermen and oilers have their cabins on the lower deck between the park and the food store. (On our ship, the second engineer and the helmsman had interchanged their berths because of the helmsman's work on the bridge.) Eating and sleeping are the two nearly exclusive activities that take place in the dining rooms and cabins. The only private space aboard is in the cabins. In a sense, the galley is an extension of the messes

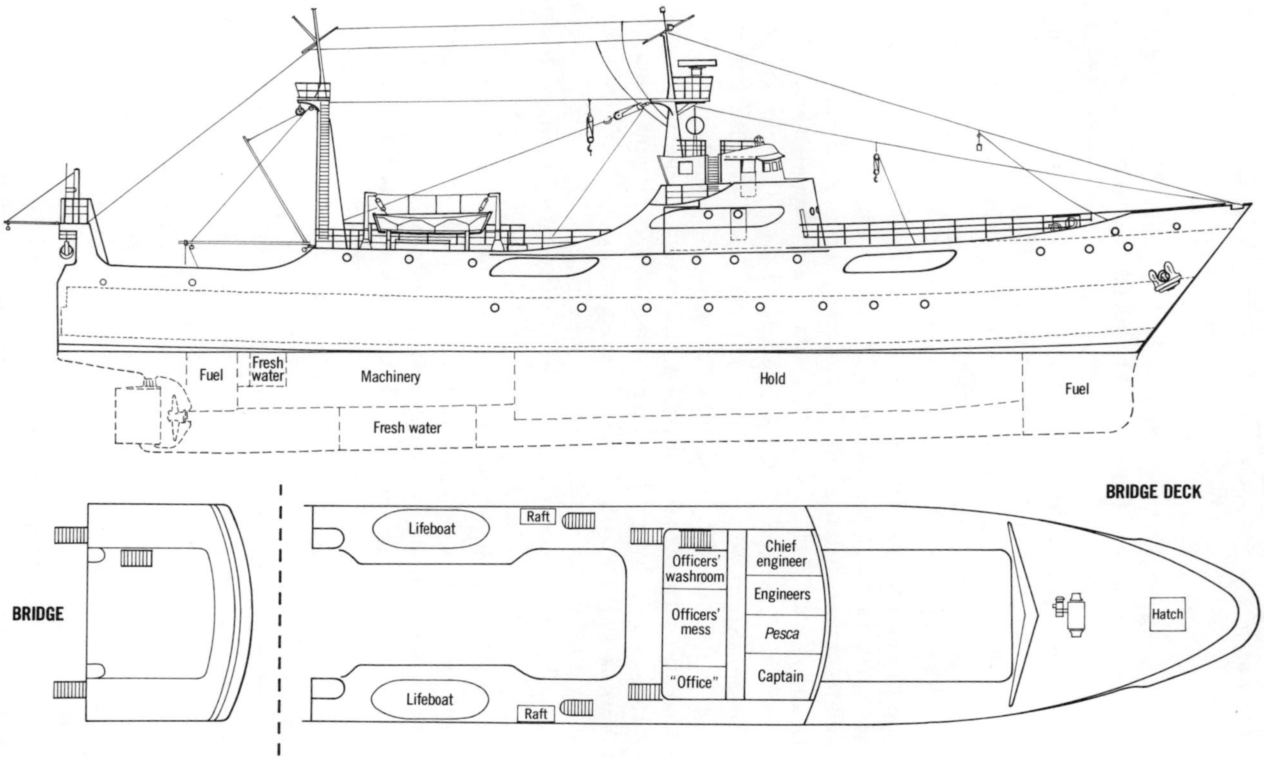

BRIDGE DECK

Hatch

Chief engineer | Engineers | Pesca | Captain
Officers' washroom | Officers' mess | "Office"

Raft | Raft
Lifeboat | Lifeboat

Fuel
Hold
Machinery
Fresh water
Fresh water
Fuel

BRIDGE

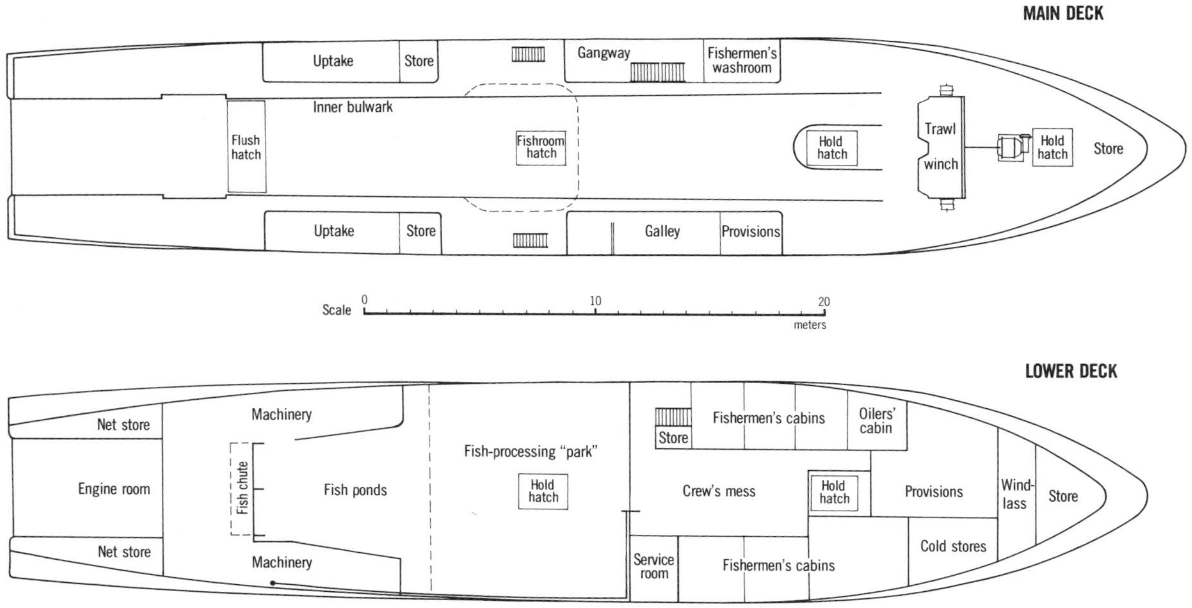

FIGURE 4
The Ship's Layout

and therefore a resting place which belongs equally to "up" and "down," in addition to the cabins.

It is worth noting that the range of leisure activities while at sea is more limited than one might expect. For example, the *pesca* and the cook told me that they liked to play cards ashore but not on board. Of the few times that I wanted to play cards at night, only once did I succeed in gathering three other fishermen. Aside from sleeping and eating, leisure time was spent talking about home and village life, reading cowboy stories or looking at pornographic magazines, and occasionally writing letters and working at handicrafts. Yet the nature of the work and the cramped quarters on board tended to mean that much of the time that was spent "resting" (for example, while waiting for a fishing operation to begin or to be completed) was not enjoyed as leisure time.

SOCIAL STRUCTURE

It has been previously stated that the captain and the *pesca* head two different authority structures and that the first *pesca* represents the owner's interests, with sole responsibility for fishing strategy. However, when it comes to the two captains, the role delineation is not as clear. In our *pareja* the captain of the first ship appeared to be responsible for the performance of the captain of the second ship; but it may happen that the only officer in the *pareja* with the status of captain is in the second ship (the first ship having a *costa* or "official"); in this case the first ship would be subordinated to the second on the basis of the formal authority structure of the *pareja* (not of the fishing authority headed by the first *pesca*). The following description is of the first ship in our *pareja*, in which both the *pesca* and the captain exercised their authority over the *pareja*.

The captain's authority is doubly validated; although appointed by the shipowner, the captain is chosen by the *pesca*—or, at least, accepted by him. His status should not be underestimated, since the institutional jurisdiction establishes him as the highest legal and administrative authority on the ship. If a situation of total incompatibility between the *pesca* and the captain should arise on board, the ultimate authority would lie with the captain.[14]

There is one territory that is under the captain's sole jurisdiction: the galley. It takes up a space not directly used in the fishing operations and is therefore outside the *pesca*'s jurisdiction. But since the *pesca* is also the second officer in command, he has jurisdiction over the galley after the captain. Also, there is one crew member over which the captain has sole jurisdiction (at least in theory) and that is the cook, who is recruited by the captain. This fact puts a strain on the relationship between the *pesca* and the cook. On our voyage the *pesca* never entered the galley, although he was frequently on deck and had to pass by the galley. Moreover, the *pesca* had a joking relationship with the cook, who told me: "Each time I go to the bridge to bring him [the *pesca*] his breakfast sandwich, he starts telling me that I treat the captain better than I do him, or something like that. He knows that I treat both of them equally, but he has to be always joking in that sense. I am always forced to run away from the bridge, and he goes on complaining even when I am gone." This was the most noticeable joking relationship aboard.[15]

The *pesca*, on his part, could take advantage of his relationship with the shipowner to show that his status on board was superior to that of the captain. This was manifest one day when the shipowner let our *pesca* know, by telegram, his decision that we should stay at sea until the end of the month. After remarking, "This is the moment I like best, interrupting his sleep," the *pesca* called the captain in a particularly abrupt manner. A moment later, in the presence of the chief engineer and myself, and while the captain was still in his cabin waking up, he shouted, "Come on, Capi, I have news for you." During supper, the *pesca* and the captain wanted to know the quantity of food left on board, and the cook had to be summoned. The problem of who should do this, the *pesca* or the captain, was resolved by a shifting of authority from the *pesca* (who announced the shipowner's decision) to the captain (who had jurisdiction over the cook) by the *pesca*'s ordering the captain (in a joking manner), "Tell the cook to come to the office [a term quite alien to a fishing ship] to receive the orders." The captain then ordered me, "Tell the cook that I want him to come here." When the cook came, the *pesca* joked with the cook about his town's football team for two or three minutes before "handing him over" to the captain. The status imbalance of the *pesca*'s position—supreme authority in most matters and lack of authority in a few others—was turned by the *pesca* into a joking relationship. Needling the cook was in fact a way of getting at the captain as well as the cook.

Besides seeing that the crew were fed (through the cook), the captain's other 'motherly' duty was the medical assistance he personally gave to crewmen suffering from a minor injury or illness. When his rudimentary medical knowledge proved insufficient, the Spanish doctor in St. Pierre or St. John's was called upon.

The *pesca*'s statement, "In harbour I am but one more fisherman," meaning "In harbour the authority belongs to the captain," is an indirect way of identifying sea and fishing as one and of confirming the *pesca*'s superiority over the captain at sea. This is supported by the fact that the location of the first *pesca* determines which ship in the *pareja* is first, regardless of the captain's location. The second trawler, as mentioned, takes orders from the first and must report her situation to the first trawler every thirty minutes.

The lines of authority, therefore, are generally clearly drawn between a *pesca* and a captain. Between two *pescas* (one on each trawler), however, the lines of authority are less clear because the second *pesca*, in his trawler, replaces the first *pesca*. This situation usually results in a predictable tendency on the first *pesca*'s part to undermine the second *pesca*'s authority by frequently humiliating him on the radio. This was not the case in our *pareja* as the *pescas* were rather friendly towards one another. I heard the first *pesca* shouting at the second *pesca* on the radio only twice, and two other occasions were reported to me. In addition, there have been cases of the first *pesca* sending his second *pesca* home from port.

Once it is understood that the division of authority falls into place according to the two functions of fishing and shipboard management, and that the time at sea is dedicated to fishing, the fishermen follow the *pesca*'s orders. The fishing strategy involves decisions about the selection of the fishing area, scheduling the manoeuvres, length of time for dragging, hauling the net in one or several drawings, the watch on the fishlupe, care of the net, maximum use of the fish taken aboard, salting and storing. Those working on the deck occupy themselves with the two phases of the manoeuvre and fish processing, while those on the bridge guide the manoeuvre and the dragging which focus the officers' attention on the fish finder as well as on the safety of the net.

Although all decisions regarding fishing strategy are exclusively the *pesca*'s, he does have to rely on the captain (or *costa*) for part of the dragging operation, which in a *pareja* can take as long as twenty-four hours, apart from the time needed for the manoeuvres and short routes. The dragging in our trawler was directed by the *pesca* by day and by the captain at night. The decision-making was strictly the *pesca*'s but the course was plotted mainly by the captain. The *pesca* directed the manoeuvres; the captain looked after those who were injured or ill. The fish-processing in the park and the salting in the hold were supervised by the *pesca*; the captain was responsible for the galley. Any interpersonal problems created because of working conditions on deck or in the park-hold were handled by the *pesca*, whereas any social disturbance in the galley or general unrest was handled by the captain.

Occasionally a captain may complain about the subordination of his role to the *pesca*'s, arguing that his duty is to steer the ship but not to conduct the draggings, which job belongs to the *pesca* and which ultimately benefits him. The cook disclosed that friction between the *pesca* and the captain is most likely to be provoked by the latter's insufficient attentiveness during the night dragging. The location of officers' quarters on our trawler reflected these status contradictions: the captain's cabin came first, the *pesca*'s second, but in the mess the *pesca* occupied the first position and the captain the second.

The officers' social relations with the fishermen were, on the whole, remarkably good on our trawler, with the exception of the final month of December, when the heavy work schedule, the *pesca*'s miscalculation in salt needs, and the uncertainty about the date of return created extreme tension that had a negative effect on the whole crew.

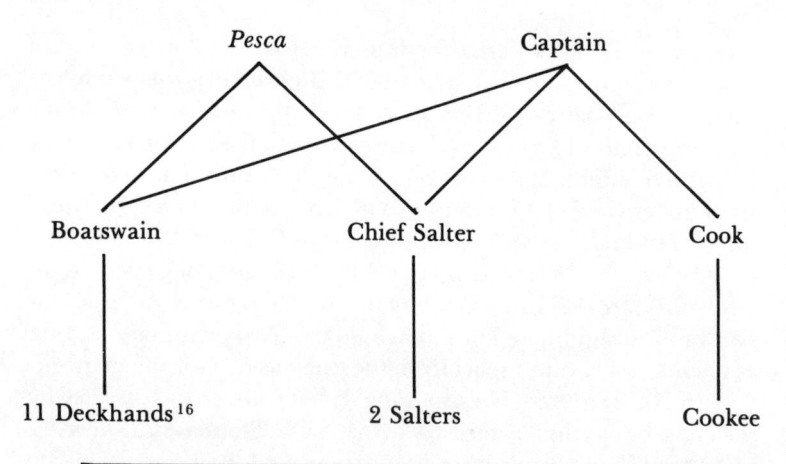

```
                Pesca              Captain
                 /\                  /\
                /  \    _____/     /  \
               /    \  /       \   /    \
              /      \/         \ /      \
         Boatswain   Chief Salter         Cook
             |            |                |
             |            |                |
     11 Deckhands[16]  2 Salters         Cookee
```

FIGURE 5
The Structural Position of the Three Petty Officers

The hierarchical distance between the officers and the fishermen is bridged on each trawler by the three petty officers: the boatswain, the chief salter and the cook, as shown in Figure 5. In general, communication at sea between bridge and deck (main deck, park) is carried out by the *pesca* and the boatswain, and between bridge and hold by the *pesca* and the chief salter.

The strategy of the manoeuvres tightens the link between the boatswain, who is responsible for the deck operations, and the *pesca*'s supervision from the bridge. The chief salter is responsible for the salting and storing of the fish. If there is any major decision to be made regarding storage in the hold, or if any personnel trouble occurs in the hold, the chief salter consults the *pesca*; but it is to the captain that he is responsible for the daily count of fish stored. The boatswain and chief salter's positions are mutually independent, so that the chief salter is not bound to be present at any of the manoeuvres or work on deck except when the net is hauled.

The boatswain's responsibility to the captain is reduced at sea to matters of personal safety and hygiene; in harbour the boatswain carries out the captain's orders regarding matters such as departure time.

I was informed that the second *pesca* usually bickers with his boatswain more frequently than does the first *pesca* with his boatswain. If this is the case, a possible reason would be that the status distance between the second *pesca* and his boatswain is shorter than that between the first *pesca* and his boatswain, so that fixed boundaries are harder to maintain.

The social boundaries of the fishermen as a group (including the three petty officers and the cookee) were set up, vertically, in opposition to the officers and engineers and, horizontally, in opposition to the oilers. The social distance between petty officers and fishermen was reduced by the friendly behaviour of the former. Moreover, the concentration of power in the *pesca* makes the petty officers' authority lose relevance; at least this was the boatswain's complaint when he assured me repeatedly that in the *bou* system the boatswain holds a considerably higher status.

The petty officers top the fishermen's group and the cookee is at the bottom, so that the fishermen themselves occupy the middle position. The cookee is called "Cho," indicating a total lack of status. (The word happens to be Basque and is used to attract anyone's attention. I was told of a Basque fisherman who, when in rage, would call everybody "Cho," thus verbally depriving them of any social status. The Galicians frequently add a diminutive to it, "Choiño," making the term even more expressive of affectionate familiarity, of the cookee's lack of status and his role as the butt of jokes.) The cookee is stereotyped as being young and an apprentice.[17]

Among the fishermen themselves, no status differences are permitted, even though there are differences in skill, experience, age, previous holding of a petty-officer position, and so on. The helmsman, although a fisherman, has the distinction of working on the bridge under the *pesca*'s direct orders, but he is frequently considered an informer and fishermen treat him with some mistrust. The three salters were graded as "chief," "second" and "third." Knowledge of the net, skill in repairing it, ability in heading and splitting either manually or with machines, endurance, awareness of danger, promptness, sociability—these are some of the qualities that are particularly appreciated in a fisherman.

If one considers continual, self-assertive, verbal confrontations as normal, then social relations among the fishermen were excellent on our trawler. The fishermen's task was a collective one: to get the fish aboard and to process it, and there were no obstacles to achieving the necessary co-operation. In addition, determination to get along was an essential factor. Although we were brought together by chance, any failure in being companions on board could turn our life into a hell. This meant that everyone had to make an effort to get along with the others.

There was friction between the boatswain and the chief salter, however, and it was caused by the role structure. It was the boatswain's task to decide which fish were too small to be processed; on the other hand, it was the chief salter's duty to report each day the number of tons put into storage (although the final figure reported to the shipowner was secretly settled by the *pesca*). It is easy to imagine the kind of problems created if the fish were small. The *pesca*, to make sure that the fishermen would not senselessly throw away too many fish, would set for the boatswain a target to be reached each day. The fishermen sometimes protested that some fish were too small to be processed.[18]

The chief salter is bound to estimate the tons stored as accurately as possible, for otherwise the *pesca* could reprimand him; consequently, the only way the boatswain could avoid the *pesca*'s dissatisfaction on the occasions when the actual number of tons of processed fish was less than the *pesca*'s estimated figure was for the chief salter to give a higher number of tons than was actually stored, something he was always reluctant to do. Thus, each time the fish caught were small, there was the potential for conflict between the boatswain and the chief salter, in spite of their friendship.

THE SOVEREIGNTY OF CUSTOM

Turning now to the regulation of the fishermen's life on board, a

The Pareja as a Social Institution

point that should be stressed (and that would take much longer to explore than the present sketch) is that, in a real sense, custom becomes law, or law is interpreted as custom.

As an example of the innumerable occasions I had to realize the sovereignty of custom, I relate the following story. During our departure from Spain, on a day when I was particularly hungry at suppertime, the cook did not allow me to eat anything in the twenty minutes between the fishermen's and officers' suppers, or after the officers had finished their supper. Not until I had washed up all the dishes and cleaned the galley did he allow me to eat. I complained in front of the crew about the irrationality of being forced to work fourteen hours straight[19] and then being compelled to be the last one to have supper, all alone. I was amazed by the crew's reaction, which I expected to be favourable to me. The officers looked at one another, surprised by my complaint; the captain came over to the galley, pointing out that he himself, when he was cookee, used to have supper last; the Basque salter, who felt morally responsible for me, was visibly upset by my early disagreement with the cook; the boatswain started cheering me up with the argument that at the time of dragging my work was much lighter than theirs; no fisherman had a word of sympathy for me.

I had to conclude that the cook could not be totally wrong, for everybody turned his back on my complaint. But how could it make sense to them that after I had served supper to the fishermen and officers, I still had to do my washing-up for another hour before I could eat? Obviously, the point was not whether I could eat supper before the washing-up or not, but whether I was conforming with the custom on board; for if the system were not respected, no social rule could govern life on board.

Since authority was cloaked in custom, and the interpretation of custom was a right connected with higher status (the cook waived my obligation to observe custom on many occasions, as a sign of friendliness), challenging a custom was the same as challenging the whole structure of authority on board. It took me days of fighting with the cook before he permitted me to sit with the fishermen while serving meals. At the beginning, the fishermen themselves were surprised by the fact that I would sit beside them, until the boatswain responded authoritatively to the general uneasiness: "Yes, man, why not; you can sit with us." The change of custom was approved by those who, a few days before, had unanimously rejected my complaint.

A description of the incidents that took place between the cook and myself, a training course of the customs on board, would be endless. To illustrate the kind of customs that governed our life, I mention some pertaining to my role as cookee in relation to the cook. I always had to wake up first; I had to finish working in the galley last; I was not allowed to eat before the cook or to sit with the fishermen at the table; I was allowed to cook breakfast only, provided I did not use other supplies except for potatoes and fish (also eggs, with the cook's permission); and so on.

The basic point the cook stressed was that I had no duties outside those given by him. He strongly opposed my doing for the fishermen any job not ordered by him; it was not my duty, for there was no custom behind it. The strongest point of his argument was always, "To do it once means to have to do it forever," or "The beginning of something is like law; afterwards they demand it from you." Much in the same way, "Once you provide a reason for complaint, you are lost, for they feel they have a right to go on complaining, no matter *how* you prepare the meals."

The ideology of custom gave the cook the right to exercise his authority over me in a supposedly impersonal way, for such was the custom and the custom had to be obeyed. On the other hand, "once means forever" implies that a social structure based on custom (alternatively rigid and changeable) tends to deteriorate and necessitates frequent renewal. At least this was the case with our *pesca* who, in his ten years of fishing in Terranova, had frequently changed second *pescas*, captains and boatswains. The case was the same with the cook, who had adopted the rule of never taking as cookee somebody who had already been a crew member with him, "because they know my weak points."

From the *pesca* to the cookee, the different fishing roles are regulated and taught by custom. Power on board is partially legitimized by customs that are accepted by the crew as necessary for keeping social order. This means that work is not regulated by direct contractual rights of labour in exchange for money, but the work itself (in addition to the external economic and paramilitary frames) has to be submitted to a social structure based on strict and hardly controllable power, as well as ruled by a system of customs that greatly obstructs any improvements of the working conditions on board. The fishermen's feeling is that ultimately, instead of legally defined rights, they are regulated solely by custom.

Several times I was assured by the fishermen themselves that "to be a fisherman is the lowest thing." Although proud of themselves, Terranova fishermen are very aware that the world does not have a high regard for their occupation. On the one hand, they have no trade union—no guaranteed continuity of employment, no settled salary, and poor working conditions; on the other hand, the circumstances of their work are rigidly controlled by paramilitary regulations.

It is not surprising, then, that the fishermen view the ship as a quite temporary institution in the sense that it does not offer them any guarantee of work continuity; the contracts of the entire crew classify them, "for all purposes, as temporary personnel." Each time a fisherman takes a job he is chosen by the *pesca* through the boatswain; this means a fisherman can, is even likely to, lose his job if any trouble with the officers occurs, or if he gets disabled, or when he becomes old. A good example of this temporariness happened on the companion trawler after our voyage. In spite of the general willingness to work on the same ship for the following voyage, only one out of the eighteen fishermen was chosen, and the *pesca* gave no reason for his total change of crew.

One implication of this demeaning status situation is that the contractual and working relations on board a *pareja* take the form of a tribal enclave inside a capitalist entrepreneurial organization. Another implication is that since legal status, in this case, does not guarantee social rights, these are defended as individual rights and personal values. In other words, rights normally associated with status become translated into the category of personal honour; since nothing is regarded as a fault against his status, anything can be offensive to his honour.

Notes

1. This is a French system of fishing where a single large trawler (*bou*) is used, and where the captain is in charge of both fishing operations and administration.
2. In the everyday estimate of tons fished on the voyage, we used to keep one account of both trawlers' catches. When we returned to home port, the salted fish stored in both holds was treated as a single amount, of which an equal percentage was shared by every crew member regardless of the catch in each ship; we had "turned over" so many million pesetas in nearly five months, and so our money was a percentage of that total figure.
3. The officers and engineers were titled "Nautical-Fishing Professional Formation" as opposed to "Officials," the difference being that those with the latter titles had attended a nautical school of university rank, whereas the former base their training mostly on experience. Our captain, with no previous high school education, had attended a nautical fishing school for three years. The *pesca*'s and chief engineer's theoretical training consisted of a nine-month course.
4. This is a tentative figure since the *pesca*'s established percentage ranges from 4 to 8 (and sometimes even more), depending on the shipowner's assessment of his worth.
5. Although the father was the owner of our *pareja*, the son was the manager of it; both were present all the time at Vigo's home port, but they were always referred to in the singular as *el Armador*, "the Armourer."
6. Due to my personal location, the ethnography in this study reflects the *pareja*'s decision-making from the first trawler and does not include the resulting actions on board the second trawler.
7. Bureaucratically (cf. the Ordinance of Work), captain-*pesca* relations have definitions other than the one discussed here, but I do not find it necessary to burden the reader with them.
8. Ley Penal y Disciplinaria de la Marina Mercante.
9. I was disapproved of by our shipowner because I was a student. This I was told by the captain, who had accepted me (rather unwillingly) because of his close friendship with a priest to whom I had outlined my plan of study.
10. Since 1963, at least eight priests have embarked on the Terranova voyages, focusing their efforts on organizing fishermen's meetings and creating public-opinion movements through the media. "Stella Maris" is an international organization whose purpose is to aid fishermen.
11. Some of the terminology used on board supports the military

The Pareja as a Social Institution

tradition in the *pareja* institution: a fisherman is a *marinero raso*, or "mere fisherman," an expression that parallels *soldado raso*, "mere soldier"; a common term for voyage is "campaign," "regulations" are *ordenanza*, and the shipowner himself is *armador* or "armourer." Many of these usages would not be understood by people on shore.

12. My own translation of Soroa.

13. Some dimensions of the ship are: maximum length, 52.10 meters; design breadth, 20 meters; gross register, 540 metric tons; net register, 207 metric tons; maximum draught, 3.82 and 4.82 meters; draught in ballast 1.70 and 4.56 meters; volume of the hold, 500 cubic meters; volume of the fuel tanks, 300 cubic meters. The capacity of each ship's hold is about 500 metric tons of processed fish.

14. In fact, this rare case did occur in 1974, and the *pesca* returned to Spain in the companion trawler, abandoning his own ship. The captain reported another case (in Angola) in which the *pesca*, drunk, threatened him physically; the captain retaliated by forbidding the *pesca* to go up to the bridge again. Although nowadays serious friction between the *pesca* and captain is highly unlikely, it was frequently the case when the *pareja* system took over and a captain who had previously commanded *bous* was forced to share his authority with a *pesca*.

15. The *pesca* also liked to needle the chief engineer with sarcastic remarks at dinnertime. Likewise, he frequently called the captain "my fellow countryman," because both were from Guipúzcoa, or familiarly *"capi"* (the abbreviation of *capitan*), which reminds one of teenage boys addressing their football coach.

16. The remaining fisherman is the helmsman, who is directly under the *pesca*'s orders on the bridge and under the boatswain on deck.

17. The national work regulations in the fishing industry, before the 1976 Ordinance, supported this stereotype in that it stated that the cookee be under 18 years old. The official word to designate the cookee's status is *marmitón* (literally, "pot"), a term used only by the cook sometimes. In my case, personal status prevailed over role status, for the crew addressed me by my own name; nevertheless, when referring to my duties, particularly if I were not present, they called me "Cho."

My holding the lowest rank created some status disturbances on the bridge, as, for example, when the captain asked me to teach him English (he lasted for two classes), or when my services were needed to call St. John's radio (this particularly was not to the *pesca*'s liking; he would soon turn it into a cause for scorn or a joke). Likewise, when we came to St. John's harbour, the fact that I knew the city and the language was immediately interpreted as my ability to get girls. This conferred on me a status enhancement quite in contradiction with my being the "Cho." Therefore, when back at sea and after each stay in St. John's, the fishermen, and particularly the officers, tried to destroy my harbour superiority, accusing me of "totally defrauding" them for not getting the girls I had promised them.

18. The processing of really small fish takes two or three times longer than processing good fish. Particularly in times of heavy work, fishermen may decide that the money they get from processing small fish does not measure up to the hours of rest it takes from them.

19. The Ordinance stipulated that under normal circumstances, work should not be prolonged beyond eight hours.

CHAPTER 2

Near and Distant Relations

Este amor apasionado	This passionate love
anda todo alborotado	goes round and round longing
por volver;	to return;
voy camino a la locura	I am on the way to madness
y aunque todo me tortura[1]	and though all tortures me
sé querer;	yet I know how to love;
nos dejamos hace tiempo	we left each other long ago
pero me llegó el momento	but now it is my time
de perder;	to lose;
tú tenías mucha razón	you were wholly right
yo hago caso al corazón	I pay attention to the heart
y me muero por volver	and I am dying to return
(CHORUS)	(CHORUS)
Y volver, volver, volver	And return, return, return
a tus brazos otra vez;	to your arms again;
llegaré hasta dónde estés	I will reach to where you are
yo sé perder, yo sé perder,	I know how to lose, I know how to lose
quiero volver, volver, volver.	I want to return, return, return.

The settings that circumscribe the fishermen's emotional life are home, ship and foreign harbour. Home is where the emotional gratification is experienced through the family and leisure time; ship is identified with deprivation of the family on the one hand and work on the other; foreign harbour represents the opportunity for deviant gratification. The interplay of these contexts shapes the for deviant gratification. The interplay of these contexts shapes the ethos of the Terranova fishermen, which is the subject of this chapter.[2] Guiding my interpretation is Bateson's definition of ethos: "The expression of a culturally standardized system of organization of the instincts and emotions of individuals" (1936: 118).

Terranova fishermen spend an average of five to seven months at sea per voyage (two voyages per year), and stay with their families from twenty to thirty days between voyages. Therefore, during approximately ten months of the year they experience their families only in fantasy. It is the length of this separation which provokes the typically projective nature of fishermen's emotional life, with the consequence that the fantasy relations with the family at sea are more significant than the actual relations on shore. The overwhelming importance of this fact should be kept in mind throughout this chapter.

Returning Home

The song that opens this chapter is a well-known modern Spanish love song; it was often heard on board—sometimes sung, at other times hummed over and over. I was told that "there are two terribly happy days at sea: the day you leave [Terranova] for Spain and the day you arrive home." In actual time the return trip takes only seven to ten days, but psychologically, "the return" begins the moment the ship leaves port for Terranova waters.

To where, in fact, does a fisherman "return"? Much of his affective life would be described in answering this question. Independent of the place or the social group to which he returns, what is of vital importance to a Terranova fisherman at sea is the feeling of returning itself, the awareness that today he is closer to that time than he was yesterday. Returning is the release from institutional and mental constraints at sea: I am away from home, but my situation of exile is somehow redeemed by my constant emotional returning.

The opposition between the sea of deprivation and the land of return tends to take on, in the fisherman's mind, the following assumptions:

1. The sea is the particular working condition that the fisherman must accept in order to make a living; the shore is the more general state of life from which the sea separates him and to which he must return.

2. The stay at sea is temporal, and only temporal limits make it bearable; the shore is a seemingly atemporal place which the fisherman leaves or to which he returns, and it is impossible to replace it with a better state of life.

3. The sea is felt to be a prison where emotional deprivation reigns; the shore is felt to be the place where emotional needs are satisfied.

4. The sea is where the fisherman gambles with what is possible; on shore there should be no uncertainty.

5. At sea, luck is all; on shore, family is all.

RETURNING TO DEPARTURE

"While you are in port you still don't feel it, but as soon as you leave port your head is full of memories," one fisherman explained. The actual deprivation of family and of the emotional life centred on it is felt to be so great that it needs to be counterbalanced by creating images of the world left behind. The most important aspect in understanding the fisherman's affective relations at sea is this mental projection, for imagination is the only means the fisherman has of recreating the emotional life he misses.

A very significant fact throughout the entire voyage was the absence of an exact time limit to it. Until three days before leaving the banks of Terranova, we were uncertain about the day the voyage was going to end; our emotional expectation was thus totally subject to the catches, which in turn influenced the shipowner's decision to let us return. The element of chance indirectly influenced our emotional gratification as well.

The easiest way to describe life on board is to pinpoint the social deprivations: no family, no sex, no home or village life, no leisure days, no ground stability, no work schedule, no religious or political participation, no communication with shore. Because life on board was despised as "not life," "not real," "a prison," the internal relationship established with the remote "real life" was given a reality of its own, to the point of potentially depriving life on board of any significance. It can be said that the presence of this distant reality was constantly shaping the fishermen's emotional expectations and creating a peculiar outlook on social relations on board. It was assumed that being at sea did not make any sense; that the community fishermen formed on board was less worthwhile than the other community on shore to which they really belonged; that therefore the mental relationship with that physically missing world was more important than any social relations on board.

"We think only of fish and home," said the cook repeatedly. "Since we don't do anything else [other than fish], neither see nor hear anything else, we necessarily have to think of the family. What else could we be thinking?" As the captain put it: "Here you are living with no other thing in your mind but those who are on shore, to earn money for them." The need for supporting the family provokes a dependence on economic luck at sea; money means luck on the one hand and emotional gratification on the other, and the family is the justification for the deprivation.

Five fishermen on our trawler were unmarried. One of them was to marry just after the voyage ended; another one had a fiancée and was likely to marry soon; the other two were young and not engaged. Only one oiler, thirty-five years old, could be considered a confirmed bachelor, and his earnings went to his mother. I had the impression that bachelors among Terranova fishermen were rare. The cook, throughout his twenty-three years in Terranova, could remember only a few. His brother was one of them, and "he was always thinking and talking about his nephews and nieces and making presents to them." Bachelorhood is regarded as an undesirable state: "Bachelors are to be pitied," said the *pesca*. They are to be pitied probably because of the difficulty they would have in projecting themselves emotionally towards shore. Moreover, without the responsibility of supporting a family, they would be deprived of the justification of suffering the harsh conditions at sea.

Since the fisherman projects his whole being to his loved ones on shore and emotionally depends on them, he expects some degree of emotional dependence on him from those he himself depends on. Without this affective reciprocity, he is likely to feel that his emotional dependence lacks an object on shore.

IDEALIZATIONS

To listen to a fisherman talk about his wife and children is a pleasant experience. "There is nothing I like more than playing with my children. When I go running with them, my wife always says, 'But you are like them!' " The captain also admitted that his greatest pleasure when he returned to shore was playing with his little baby, adding: "Well, with the little one and with the big one." Others confessed the same family-oriented sentiment: "Every time I go to sleep I like to remember my wife and children and the moments we had together." Some fishermen had pictures of their wife and children on the wall beside their bunk—the only private spot on board; others hung their wedding ring alongside their bunk.

Officers and fishermen alike talked about their families. During the first days of sailing, the captain repeated emphatically, "First comes the family, the rest follows." I deliberately tempted them: "Why is it that all you sailors get married when you are going to be at home, at most, two months a year? It would have been better if you remained bachelors." They reacted with laughter. This proposition was so contrary to their self-image that it could not be a threat to them. The captain jokingly added, "That is the reason why some come to sea—because they are married."

Each time the captain talked to me about his life at sea, he invariably summarized all his motivations in the statement "I am here to support my family." He and the chief engineer could even be embarrassingly sentimental when talking about their wives and were capable of doing so for periods of twenty to thirty minutes. When the captain phoned his wife and only daughter on her first birthday, the little daughter called him *Aita* (Daddy). "She called me *Aita*! She called me *Aita*!" he exclaimed the whole day. When I joked about it he answered, "But do you know what it means, that she called me *Aita*?"[3] We all celebrated her birthday with a bottle of cognac.

The *pesca* was not sentimental in talking about his wife and family, and yet he admitted that his duty to support his family was the reason for his staying at sea. On the previous voyage, when he had a better radio system and could call directly to Spain, he used to talk to his wife nearly every second day. He insisted that "what makes life at sea so hard is the separation from your family" and that this separation seemed to cause a greater need for affection while at home.

The boatswain described the day of return in this way: "For me, to be back at home is a new honeymoon. There are no words to express the happiness. The wife and children come to receive you. The children call you 'Daddy' and cry, and I cry, and that day everything is just great. It feels like the day you marry, or like an astronaut feels when he reaches the moon for the first time, with the difference that he can reach it only once, whereas a fisherman has it happen every five or six months. I have been working as a fisherman for three years now and the pleasure I get the day I go home now, after these months at sea, has nothing comparable to it in those three years. . . . You see, the fisherman has only that small bit of happiness, but he enjoys it more than other people would enjoy a life of constant pleasure. . . . It is like a woman; when she is too easy, you don't appreciate her as much as you do when it is rather difficult, even if she's not so pretty."

The last point was expressed by others as well. "It seems to me that on shore people are more selfish," remarked one fisherman, referring to the fact that people living on shore miss the emotional excitement a fisherman enjoys when at home, "as if it were always new." Similarly, the captain, upon receiving a photograph of his little daughter walking, commented, "If you are on shore, you don't appreciate what a photo like this means; only at sea do you fully know what it's worth." He liked to quote a priest friend of his who said that "a fisherman has more than 50 percent of his matrimonial problems solved, because each time he comes home he is on a new honeymoon."

MORE THAN JUST LETTERS AND SONGS

The importance of letters from home cannot be overestimated. They are virtually the only means of communication for the ten months of each year that a fisherman is away from his wife and family. On our trawler, for example, there was a fisherman who was so disturbed by the fact that he had not received a letter from his wife in the first month and a half of his stay at sea that he stopped sending her his monthly checks. When he called her from port later, at the captain's insistence, he found out that she was ill.

Fishermen are so dependent on letters that one of the criteria for judging a *pesca* is how quick he is about going to meet the trawlers that are carrying mail from Spain. Since this might entail several hours of sailing, it is not always on the priority list of some *pescas*.

Of course, in these letters the men like to receive news that reassures them of their place in the hearts of those at home. But this is not always the case; news of a wife's going to a wedding and being forced to dance with somebody, or of a wife's having a glass of wine with a male friend, can cause great emotional turmoil.

Apart from letters, the fishermen look forward to their visits in port to phone home, some of them every day. Buying gifts for the wife and children is another means of emotional contact.

Communal singing seems to be another means of indirectly communicating with the homeland and loved ones. "Singing is like getting drunk; you can do it out of sorrow or out of contentment," explained one fisherman. The words of songs perform the functions of taking the men back home, as well as uniting them in a bond of friendship; they are literally "in the same boat" and are able to share their emotions through song. It was not unusual for a group of men to sing and drink for hours on end while in port. "When I am in port I like singing. It makes me happy, I enjoy it terribly." Free from the dependence on luck and the institutional constraints at sea, affective relations in port assume the priority they have in fishermen's lives generally.

Singing often accompanied drinking sessions. In December, when the possibility of returning home was real, the boatswain made this remark to me: "The day we leave for Spain, you and I have to be singing until we are at the point of falling down exploding." And some days later he said, "The day we leave for Spain, we have to throw Julio [his cabinmate] out of the cabin and be singing and drinking, if not whiskey at least wine, until we fall down sick." Both singing and getting drunk were celebrations of contentment, carried out in an enhanced emotional state, with the additional result of uniting in friendship the people who participated in them. When the voyage was over, I stayed in various villages for fifteen days, where I could see that singing retained its important function of emotional release. It could be said that since the efficient functioning of the economic order was assured by the activity of working itself, in a similar way the performance of singing was needed to bring out the communality offered by the affective order.

THE FISHERMAN'S DILEMMA

All these emotional projections are, of course, idealizations. In point of fact, the psychological mortgage a fisherman has to pay for his long months of isolation at sea can hardly be fully described. The effects of this fishing gamble cannot be erased in twenty to thirty days at home. His difficulties in adapting to shore are enormous. While at sea all he knows is nets and fish, all he thinks of is luck and family—no newspapers, no radio, no television for months. According to a statistical poll (D.I.S. 1972), 60 percent of the fishermen felt that their own children looked upon them as strangers. According to the same poll, more than 50 percent of their wives did not like their husband's work.

"What conversation can I have with somebody living on shore? I started going to weekly dinners with some of my shore friends, and I had to stop going because I did not have anything to talk about." "Have you ever read a newspaper two days old, or one day? I ask my family to keep the daily newspapers for the time I get back, and I spend hours and hours reading them, to be up-to-date; they look at me in surprise and ask, 'But how can you be reading a newspaper two months old?' " Men as intelligent and sociable as the *pesca* would avoid meeting a friend in a *taberna*: "They will think I don't want to be with them on account of my position, but I just don't know what to say." The stories are many, the result is the same: an extreme sense of psychological alienation prevents the Terranova fisherman from feeling that life on shore belongs to him also.

The *pesca* confessed to me: "After not resting for several years, and after the shipwreck last March, I decided to stay home until July or August. When fifteen days had gone by I could not stand the thought that I was going to remain on shore for four or five months. It even makes you think there is something wrong with you." Another fisherman confessed: "At home, the last time, they were surprised that after a month on shore I was not nervous and [not] willing to go to sea. This time I stood the time on shore much easier because I had a niece with whom I could play."

The transition from life at sea, which is based on challenging the unpredictability of luck (the subject of the following chapter), to the predictable sameness of life on shore is at the root of much of the difficulty experienced by the fishermen. "I am a gambler, I like to bet," said one to me. "They [the government] gave me 22,000 pesetas (about $300) a month for unemployment. Although I would use it for food and so on, I never thought that was money; real money for me is earned at sea." The best description of the psychology underlying life at sea came from an old fisherman. "Like the water slowly filters through the walls of the hold, while the cod gets dry, so it happens with luck entering your head. I can see that, because before becoming a fisherman, I was a farmer." A good explanation for the preference for a life at sea came from our cook, who had refused several work offers from restaurants near his home, "because I would not know how to deal with people." He had treated fishermen with "motherly care" for years, but shipboard relations were substantially different from relations ashore. Other fishermen had also refused opportunities to work on shore, and the case of the fisherman who does not need to work any longer but goes on fishing "because I get bored on shore" is classical. The fact that fishing might very well be a psychological necessity for some men becomes apparent in the captain's story about his father, who left his job at sea at his mother's request. His late mother's only piece of advice to the captain's wife had been, "Don't ever force your husband to retire from the sea. The greatest wrong I did in my life was to force my husband to work on shore; he was never happy at the factory, and a lot of troubles could have been avoided if he had stayed at sea."

Therein lies the dilemma: a fisherman's thoughts turn homeward while he is at sea, but he finds them turning to the sea again once he is home. The Terranova fisherman has no place where his body and mind are one. The ever-renewed distance he is trying to bridge slowly becomes a necessary condition for his emotional gratification.

Foreign Harbour

Time in port, away from the constraints of shipboard life, was felt to be an unsolicited break which the men had to accept and enjoy; it was never regarded as a reward for work. The only reward for labour was the return home after a successful voyage. The five times we went into port were caused either by the need for repairs to the trawlers, by illness, or by a labour dispute, and not by the crew's need for rest. Each time the captain advised: "If anybody has some physical ailment or toothache, this is the time to go see the doctor." Another feature of these visits to port was the unknown time limit allotted to them. As a result, each time was regarded as "almost over," and hence as a precious and vaguely illicit gift rather than a right. You are never quite sure when the ship will depart. The first night you tell your woman that you can see her the next evening but the one after that probably not, although, in the end, you might stay a whole week and each day would be the last.

A well-known characteristic of the sailors' life (making them subjects of romantic stories) is commonly expressed in the saying "a girl in every port." To anybody unaware of seamen's sexual ideology, it might be surprising that the same man who, on board, talks at length about his wife, in port goes with the first prostitute who comes along; or that the one who boasts about his advances to a woman while dancing the night before, ends his story with the conclusion, "All that, compared with my wife, is just shit."

"In theory, she [the wife] has the same rights as the man, but . . . " But the differences in their circumstances during ten months of the year generate the conviction that wives must be faithful to their fishermen-husbands while they are away. When the cook rebuked the fishermen for this double standard, their replies were of this sort: "We are not equal—otherwise let *them* come to Terranova if they have the same rights, and we shall take care of the children"; or simply, "We need to let ourselves go." In other words, it is justifiable for a fisherman not to be faithful to his wife, but his wife has to be unconditionally faithful to him. This formulation, rather than being a justification of the occasional 'fall,' is a conceptual pattern embedded in the fisherman's ideology, the sense of which dictates its actualization in concrete behaviour.

The extent to which a double sex standard is condoned by Terranova fishermen is impressive to anyone unaware of the factors shaping their ideology. What is interesting here, more than the existence of a *macho* ideology among seamen, are the occupational features of fishing that reinforce such an ideology. An analysis of this ideology can be attempted by means of different approaches. The one I have chosen is to examine the dichotomy surrounding the fishermen's lives: the sea is the institutional reality and the shore the non-institutional reality; the transition from sea to shore automatically excludes the institutional situation. An ever-present characteristic of the seamen's culture is the tendency to isolate one arm offered by this dual environment. On the level of cognition both worlds are experienced simultaneously, but as cut off one from the other. No matter how well the voyage is going, sea means constraint; no matter what is waiting at home, shore means freedom and pleasure. Sea is prison, shore is paradise. Some elements that define this double reality are:

Sea	*Shore*
no land	land
no ground stability	stability
no leisure	leisure
no sex	sex

When the seaman arrives in port, the change from a world of deprivation to a world of full enjoyment takes place and he finds himself compelled to seek pleasure.

Wives, however, do not experience this polarity. They enjoy, so fishermen believe, the very things of which fishermen are deprived. How then could wives justify their unfaithfulness? What is worse, for wives the possibility of sex is within their reach at all times (they do not even have to worry about their husband's presence), whereas fishermen do not have the same possibility at sea. Hence sex in port corrects this inequality of opportunity; since the ship subjects fishermen to a situation of no sexual opportunity, they feel justified in correcting the situation while in port. But wives have to compensate for their privileged position of not being forcefully deprived by *not* making use of it, for if a wife were to make use of her opportunity, the discrepancy would become intolerable for every married fisherman.[4]

The key to understanding this justification of the double standard may lie in the conceptual differentiation of purely physical sex and conjugal sex supposedly based on love: the fisherman can remain a loving husband even though he has sexual intercourse with a prostitute. In addition, infidelity in a foreign port and infidelity in the home port are clearly differentiated, as indicated by a statement made by the cook: "The greatest fall that anybody could have is to be unfaithful on shore on the way back home, while wife and children are waiting for him; that is an unpardonable fall. It is not the same offence as in harbour. If you are unfaithful in St. Pierre, you have time to repent, but if you are unfaithful on shore, you have no time to repent; that would be the end. Everything needs its time." In other words, sex with a prostitute in a foreign port is a "sanctioned deviation" (Faris 1968), but not so extra-marital sex in the home port, for there is no justification for it. Shore, and all that it represents, has been reached.

The hardship of his life at sea can easily inspire the fisherman's belief that his lot is almost exclusively work, physical suffering and isolation from home, whereas the wife's is to benefit from the advantages of shore. Above all, she can enjoy the company of the children and relatives and a freedom to choose the persons who make up her network of social relations, all of which the fisherman does not have. Moreover, the fisherman's affective dependence on wife and family is too obvious, and in return he needs the reassurance of knowing that his family is emotionally dependent on him. In this framework of relations, the wife's fidelity is symbolically enhanced as the social fact *sine qua non* of her affection for him. He shows his by the working conditions he puts up with, but her emotional dependence on him is uncertain unless she guarantees complete sexual fidelity.[5] However, the fishermen are troubled on exactly this point of their wives' sexual fidelity; as one fisherman put it, "The wife is mentally unfaithful, even if not physically." And it is because of this circumstance that a fisherman can find himself enmeshed in a double-bind kind of situation (Bateson 1972). On the one hand, to remain sexually faithful while in port is to underwrite his *disadvantaged* position compared to his wife's; but on the other hand, to go to a prostitute is to admit implicitly that his wife is—or at least is free to be—unfaithful to him.

Shipboard Social Relations

Although the strongest emotional ties of the fishermen are with their families on shore, dependency relations do develop among the individuals thrown together by the institutional structure of the ship. As mentioned previously, relations between fishermen themselves, and between officers and fishermen, were excellent on our trawler. The cook remarked several times that in his twenty-three years of fishing in Terranova, he could hardly remember a voyage in which "people got along so well with each other." What follows is an analysis of the mechanisms that contributed to the harmonious relations on board our trawler.

THE COOK AND THE GALLEY

"Ninety percent of the rows come from the galley," the *pesca* pointed out to me early in the voyage. That such a high proportion of conflict could stem from the galley's incompetence (which, in the case of the companion trawler, proved to be so) presents an interesting fact with which to begin a description of the social relations on board.

When I first heard this figure I did not believe it could be true, for it seemed unlikely that cooks, such as the one we had, whose competence and understanding contributed greatly to the well-being of the crew, could be the source of so much disturbance. However, after I discussed this with the cook, it became clear that his job carried much responsibility. The cook was surprised at my question as to whether he had experienced discontent with his cooking. "Of course. On the last voyage they all protested about my meals at a certain time; the captain had to talk to the fishermen." When asked what kind of meals he had prepared then, he replied, "Like now, completely the same," and explained that "when you are fishing well there are no problems, but if there is no fish. . . ." The captain, on one occasion, commented that after some time at sea "You get so fed up with everything that you just want a change. You prefer an old sardine to a good chop."

The cook was sceptical each time I flattered him with the crew's satisfaction with his meals: "You don't know these people. I know them well." In fact, he went through several periods of depression, feeling insecure about satisfying the crew's expectations. On at least three occasions he literally begged for my mediation between himself and the fishermen, for he was "not sure whether the people are content." He once confessed to me that he had been so worried he was unable to sleep for several nights. This was a man who had been a cook in Terranova for twenty-three years, who claimed ours was one of the best crews he had ever known, and who had been praised numerous times as being one of the best cooks in the whole Terranova fleet. It was certainly not the lack of competence that would give rise to so much anxiety on the part of the cook and potential unrest on the part of the crew.

The number of times both officers and fishermen declared that the cook was "the soul of the ship" led me to regard this statement as the shipboard definition of the cook's status. "He is like our mother," was another common expression. The cook himself had internalized this role, for his advice to me the first night I met him was: "It is not enough just to serve the food; it is necessary to serve it in a certain way so that the fishermen will feel good. Our duty is not only to provide food; we have to be kind and understand their moods when they come from the deck in a bad temper."

The galley was the place that seemed most like a home. It provided fire and food—beyond the reach of the smell of fish. On our trawler, however, the galley was badly located, a fault which provoked constant amazement and blame. One had to cross the deck to get to it and in the Terranova winter, this meant having to wear boots and perhaps deck clothing. The cook himself, accustomed to wearing slippers at sea, expressed his indignation about the galley's location: "A cook with boots!"

Fishermen had only occasional access to the galley during the cook's working hours, for he would not allow them to remain in his territory. But during the cook's time off, particularly during the night, nobody would say a word if one of the crew went into the galley and prepared a meal for himself. On days when there was no work, it was rare if someone was not cooking a snack for three or four people. If it were not some tasty tidbit that the net had provided, such as halibut or redfish, a special dish would be offered; a different part of the cod, an omelette, squid, a canned delicacy, or even a steak that the cook had neglected to hide.

As the voyage approached the end, the cooking activity of the fishermen became almost a daily happening, always regretted but tolerated by the cook.[6] At first it astounded me that after a lunch of up to three bowls of soup and a heavy stew at 11:30, to be followed by a dinner of another three dishes of soup, fish and meat at 6 P.M., the men could cook and eat an in-between snack at 3 P.M.; or that they could wake up at 5 A.M. to have a breakfast of salted redfish.

Obviously it was not hunger but the emotional connotations of cooking that moved them: "Even if my cooking is worse than the cook's, there is a special pleasure in cooking for myself," said one fisherman who, on the previous voyage, used to wake up each midnight when not working to prepare "some special dish." Cooking functioned as a way of restoring the feeling of home. In contrast to eating at scheduled times, in forced company and without choice in the selection of food, one's own cooking was voluntary and unstructured. On board, a fisherman could never go for a walk, or go to a lounge for a drink, or share a meal in a restaurant with his friends. Instead, he could go to the galley, cook something and share it with some of his companions together with a bottle of special wine.

Similarly, the fifteen-minute pause for refreshment—a half-glass of vermouth—before lunch every day was observed with the strictness of a ritual. Apart from being a *rite de passage* from work (institution) to eating (home), it served as a substitute for the drinks customarily had in village bars before going home for dinner.

The figure quoted by the *pesca*, that 90 percent of the rows come from the galley, is obviously exaggerated; nevertheless, it reflects the extent to which potential conflict centres around the territorial and functional unit most loaded with emotional meaning. Regardless of whether discontent stems from overwork (when there are too many fish) or boredom (when there are no fish), and even though both conditions are cognitively attributed to luck, the fishermen tend to relieve their frustrations in the part of the institutional structure that offers "motherly" care, the galley. The cook was right to be sceptical about the fishermen's unpredictable reactions towards him, even though his cooking was consistently good. This scepticism is general among all the cooks coming to Terranova. The conclusion is that there is a tendency to centre any feelings of unrest in the galley.

UNWRITTEN RULES OF BEHAVIOUR: DEPENDENCY AND SELF-ASSERTION

The collective experiencing and controlling of emotions is essential for maintaining harmony on board ship. No one can claim personal reasons for being in a mood different from the mood of the whole group. The main factors determining the prevailing mood on board (apart from proximity to port or home) are the fishing moment, the fulfillment of each person's role, and the interaction between the different groups. *Ser un amargado*, "to be embittered," is the contemptuous phrase applied to any crew member who is upset or who hides some resentment. "What wrong has been done to this man?" I heard the boatswain ask more than once, referring to the chief engineer. "If he is an embittered man, let him stay away from the sea."[7] Likewise, a good mood on board ship has to be experienced collectively.

Meal times normally bring together, as well as bring to attention, emotion and attitudes. Isolation, threats and personal attack are the means of sanctioning unacceptable behaviour. Group control is reinforced by the awareness that any member can cause, by his deviant behaviour, a total disturbance and even force work to stop. Behaviour that is not tolerated, besides inappropriate moods, includes non-acceptance of authority, personal attack, refusal to work, and incompatibility with some other crew member.

The dependence of crew stability on each individual's sound behaviour makes everyone responsible for everybody else's welfare: if a fisherman does not have an appetite for a meal, it may mean that he is not going to yield as much work as he could in the next working period; if an engineer is ill, it means that the other five men in the engine-room will have their work altered; if somebody is in danger of having a mental breakdown, this implies a collective threat. One fisherman told me how scared he was on his previous voyage because of two men who, on one occasion, had thrown their knives at somebody.

The nature of the work and life aboard a fishing trawler greatly stresses the mutual interdependence of its parts: bridge and deck; bridge-deck and engine-room; deck and park; park and hold; galley and bridge-deck-engines. This dependence extends internally to the members of each group—the two officers, the three engineers, the three oilers, the two galley workers, the twelve deckhands, the three salters—and together they form a structural and functional unit which needs the full collaboration of each member.

Contrary to what one may expect, self-assertive verbal behaviour seems to be a necessary mechanism for maintaining equilibrium on board. This usually takes the form of noisy arguments about trivial matters, adopting provocative attitudes towards one another, and an inclination to boasting. A fisherman complaining angrily that he was left alone cleaning the park, or arguing that the tons of fish stored are more than the chief salter's note says, or adamantly asserting that a certain football team has four foreign players and not three, or arguing aggressively with six others as to whether the English or Chinese language is more widely spoken in the world—these are all typical ways of communicating and have nothing to do with personal enmity. Similarly, noisy rows break out as a matter of course if something goes wrong in a manoeuvre.

The way in which orders are given illustrates the aggressive nature of shipboard communication. For example, if the *pesca* has to communicate from the bridge window to the boatswain that something is going wrong during a manoeuvre, he will likely need to yell or even swear.[8] Our boatswain was a remarkably kind man; yet at any moment he might have to assert his authority to the men: "I am the one who commands on deck during the manoeuvres, and not the *pesca*. You must do what I order, and nothing else." Once I happened to be by his side on deck while he was yelling to the fisherman in charge of the winch to let go the bridles. He realized I was there and, smiling, said: "I shout but I have a good heart, don't you think so?"

As described in Chapter 3, the *pesca*'s hold over the fishermen was charismatic, stemming from his mediation with luck. However, as the end of the voyage drew near, this charismatic relationship suffered a noteworthy change. Having achieved a good catch of fish, and feeling assured of his supreme status on board, the *pesca* developed a rather provocative attitude in his relations with the captain in particular and the fishermen in general. His attitude showed a lack of concern for the fishermen's welfare. But the fishermen were able to distinguish between the decisions he made while he was dependent on luck and those that were merely arbitrary demands on them. The following incident shows the potential damage that can result in the relationship of trust between the *pesca* and the fishermen. Before leaving Spain, the *pesca* made a mistake in loading too much salt on board. Later, in the middle of the longest working period of the whole voyage, he ordered the fishermen to shovel the tons of surplus salt overboard. When, after another ten days of exhausting fish-processing, the fishermen were ordered to throw more salt overboard, they bitterly criticized the *pesca* for the first time.

The humiliation arose not from the work itself, but from the fact that in the *pesca*'s opinion, the fishermen's exhaustion was not a consideration. He could have altered the casting turn once and, while the men were working on the salt, ordered the companion trawler to shoot their net; or he could have stopped fishing for one day while the crew were working in the hold; or he could have delayed repairing the net, for it was not absolutely necessary. The fishermen went as far as to suggest that the *pesca*, since the fault was his, could have hired harbour workers in St. Pierre to throw out the surplus salt.

At the end of the voyage, our social relations were no longer controlled by the uncontrollable factor of luck; the sudden intensification of feelings for home, on the occasion of Christmas, seemed to be rescuing us from the fishing ideology of luck and the *pesca*'s charismatic decision-making.

GROUP LOYALTY VERSUS PRIVATIZATION OF SOCIAL RELATIONS

Another element of behaviour that features strongly in the relationships among fishermen is jealousy. I became the object of unexpected scenes in late October when we came into St. John's for the third time, and I began to realize that any privatization of social relations was a serious threat to the group as a whole.

The first indication that something was amiss came from the lack of response to my need for help in the galley the first days in port. When I complained, one fisherman shouted at me, "I will not help you anymore!" When I asked him why he was angry with me, he replied, "You humiliated me," and walked away. The same evening, the boatswain stopped me on my way to fetch potatoes with his hand on my chest, and at the same time he and another twelve men started shouting at me, "You have abandoned us," "You are ashamed of us," "You don't even come to sing with us," "You don't even greet us," and threatened, "You will not be our friend anymore." As the startling and vociferous performance went on, I remained serious. Then one of them whispered to me, "It is a joke." But as soon as I smiled, the accusations resumed for several more minutes. When they became silent, I shouted, "You are damn fools," and they laughed.

For a better appreciation of the scene, it should be pointed out that part of my spare time in St. John's harbour was spent at the university or with a girlfriend, whom I had met while I was a student at Memorial. After that evening's verbal punishment I thought that would be the end, but I was mistaken. After dinner I stayed on board alone, then left the ship to see my friend, convinced that I had not been seen by anybody. The moment of truth occurred after lunch the next day, when somebody revealed my previous night's departure, provoking again the whole drama of the evening before.

What was the explanation for this possessive behaviour towards me when it was common practice for any of the men to have relations with the prostitutes in port, and to stay away from the ship the whole night, or even the entire period in port?[9] Understanding this seeming contradiction requires another look at the fishermen's emotional relationships. Love and affection were exclusive to life on shore with wife and family, whereas relationships in port were purely sexual—a necessary antidote for their life of deprivation on board. My enjoying an emotional relationship in port with a girlfriend in St. John's (where I had lived before and where I was returning after the voyage) was the equivalent to their relationship with their wife and as such was a threat to this pattern. I was emotionally committed while at sea (as opposed to shore) to a relationship that should be experienced only *in absentia* during the voyage (including visits in port).

Furthermore, the fishermen intentionally kept exclusive relations of a private nature within the family structure. The corollary of this tendency is that since family belongs to shore, so do all private relationships. Just as the men distinguish between purely physical sex (in port) and conjugal sex (on shore), so there seems to be a qualitative differentiation between private relations (family) and comradely relations (shipboard). The institutional structure allows for sex in port and comradeship on board as long as exclusive relationships and sex based on affective relations are absent. The important consequence of the fact that I could be enjoying at sea (in harbour) an exclusive relationship was that my emotional bonds with the crew were threatened, and this in turn threatened crew solidarity.

Their shows of jealousy were a warning that I should be aware of the implicit affective structure on board, according to which they had emotional rights over me. Because I showed my emotional independence of them, they felt humiliated and rejected. Their reactions might be based on this logic: we offer him appreciation and companionship as fishermen, but he rejects this offer because he is enjoying a private relationship with a girlfriend.

Later in the voyage we were forced to enter the port of St. Pierre. There I could not go out much with the fishermen either; however, no protests were made, for there I did not have a girlfriend.

Although I may have been the centre of emotional competition as a result of my marginal position in the affective and institutional structure of the ship, shows of jealousy were by no means absent among the fishermen themselves. One evening the fishermen insisted that I sit down and listen to "the story of the *sarda*" (*sarda* is a fish frequently eaten but not particularly liked). Amidst much laughter and joking they related the following event. One of the fishermen cooked himself a *sarda* and while eating it, gave some to another fisherman. This upset a third man, who had previously asked for a piece. To add to the offence, the first fisherman in the story gave yet another piece to the boatswain. The offended man, in retaliation, threatened to withhold his wine container from the offender (the containers had to be shared), who in turn replied that he would not drink from it for the rest of the voyage.

The men who insisted on telling me this story, turning it into a "how a fisherman almost had to take out his knife to defend his rights," were precisely those involved in the dispute. This play on jealousy, although insignificant in itself and a joking matter to the participants, had a specific sense which was understood by them and which, first of all, needed actualization in the scene that took place, and then conversion into an important story which imperiously needed to be told. Again, dramatization was used to express the emotional structure according to which no privatization of relationships was allowed on board. The undue preference for giving a piece of *sarda* to a companion when somebody else had previously asked for it (although everybody knows that it probably occurred as a slip) was adequate reason to perform a drama and even make a story out of it. The implicit emotional relations on board were deliberately exaggerated at the level of fiction.

This same sense lay at the heart of the possessive behaviour apparent in the occasional complaint made by a fisherman when I (unintentionally) did not sit in front of, or beside, him. There were similarly motivated complaints when I inadvertently served a meal to somebody "in a way you don't serve me." These complaints support the only advice I repeatedly received from two Spanish seamen living in St. John's, when I told them about my impending job aboard a Spanish trawler: "Be equal friends with everybody. Don't ever be more friendly with one than with another." The cook also advised me to bring coffee to the fishermen who were working in the park as well as to those on deck, so as "not to get them jealous." Once I served bottled wine of my own to the fishermen who were on deck taking the salt from the hold; the fishermen working down in the hold realized it and made disappointed comments, and before I could get down to offer them some (that was my intention from the beginning), the chief salter took out his wine and ostentatiously began offering it to the fishermen working in the hold.

A fact that supports the non-privatization of social relations at sea is the almost total absence of homosexuality among Terranova fishermen. I was told of only one case in which two fishermen, who had flown from Spain to join a trawler that was short of crew, were sent back when their homosexuality was discovered. The fishermen's sexual pattern of no sex on board but deviant heterosexual sex in port and conjugal sex at home was in direct opposition to the probable homosexual pattern of sex on board, deviant homosexual sex in port and no conjugal sex at home.

Other ways of avoiding privatization were in evidence on the trawler. There was the custom of leaving one's cabin door open day and night. The oilers' cabin and the cook's cabin (and mine) were the only two that usually remained closed, causing disapproval on the part of the fishermen. Many times, when I closed my cabin door to go to sleep or to write my notes while fishermen were in the mess hall, from which there were doors to all cabins, I sensed that I was performing an act of personal exclusion from the group. Some of them actually asked me, "Why do you close the door?" I would not dare close the door, however, when another fisherman was with me. It was customary not only to have the door open but also to have the light on at night. The reason for this was "because of the danger of fire." It was rather funny to hear about this precaution from the same fishermen who, after two months of sailing, did not check to see whether there was a fire extinguisher on board. The taboos against closed doors and extinguished lights clearly suggest the distaste for privacy and perhaps even a fear of exclusion.

It is significant that, in the captain's opinion, jealousy is the first symptom of mental breakdown among fishermen. Pathological jealousy is manifested in a number of ways. With regard to their wives, disturbed fishermen react abnormally to their letters and phone calls; with regard to the officers on board, they feel abandoned and attempt to ingratiate themselves; with regard to their fellow fishermen, some feel so grievously rejected that they develop persecution mania.

Epilogue: "Being a Fisherman"

"It is the suffering of the poor, you know. If you are born from a rich cunt, you are okay. If you are born from a poor cunt, you have to be like this. Some people have too much, other people nothing. You see, some people have whatever they want from generation to generation, and we others, we'll always be like this." This was the boatswain's reply when I commented on his being on deck repairing the net for hours in extremely cold weather. "The suffering of the poor" reflects the humiliation involved in being forced to become a fisherman. Each time I asked, "What other work could you do on shore?" the answer was: "I could not go to school and learn some profession" or "By tradition my family were all fishermen" or "There is no other work in my village." The respondent might even add: "To be a fisherman is the lowest thing. When you're no good for anything else, you become a fisherman." Like any migrant worker (this is another remote but real work possibility) far away from home, the fisherman feels his own estrangement; he has to choose a life which, he tells himself every day, "is not life." If he is still young, he hopes that better opportunities for work will arise, such as on some distant drilling ship in Australia, or in factories at home. If a man has spent years in the occupation of fishing, then it is possible that he will continue being a fisherman until retirement. But, according to the cook, "I have known, in twenty-three years of coming to Terranova, very, very few fishermen who reached retirement age." Coastal fishing and the merchant marine are the alternatives, providing easier but less profitable work.

The sense of humiliation makes a fisherman extremely sensitive to any gesture that indicates contempt towards him for being a fisherman. Take, for example, this common occurrence: A fisherman arrives in a port and wants to buy a camera. He enters a shop, he feels the salesgirl is looking down on him, he wants to run away; he does not know English but he keeps on asking questions; he finally decides to buy the camera, the girl makes up the bill, but there is a 10 percent tax and he says angrily that on another occasion he was not forced to pay tax and that he will not pay it. She shows him an official paper stating that the 10 percent is obligatory even for fishermen; he leaves the camera and goes out in a rage—everybody wants to exploit him. Later on he goes to another shop, where again they say that the 10 percent is legal. This time he pays the tax and buys the camera. He goes on board and tries to impress his companions with the purchase to help convince himself that he has not been cheated. Or this scene: A sick fisherman goes to see a doctor, and is asked if he can speak English, to which the medical assistant present responds with a smile on his face: "He is a fisherman." He goes back on board and relates the incident to his fellow fishermen; they all feel insulted and curse the assistant.

On board, too, they are all fishermen, or fishermen who became engineers or officers, or oilers who were fishermen and might be so again. Even so, the status of "being a fisherman" divides the crew in two: fishermen on one side, officers and engineers-oilers on the other. Fishermen are sure to react angrily if the chief engineer warns those in the park, where he has no authority, to be careful of dropping the fish scraps on the deck. The boatswain on the other ship will purposely be late by several hours at the time of leaving harbour if, although everyone knows the hour of departure, he is not personally notified by the captain, as is the rule.

"Behind all human action there is always fear," contended the *pesca*. Every accident in a manoeuvre was a reminder that "our lives are hanging from a thread." Toughness and constant verbal confrontation characterize fishermen's exterior behaviour, and yet deep inside lies hypersensitivity and prevailing uncertainty. Although open confession or show of fear is ordinarily suppressed and regarded as weakness, a treacherous sea in a bad storm could make a man who had been coming to Terranova for more than twenty years cry out in fear. Although resistance to physical pain is taken for granted, bringing one's pain to the group's attention is the first means of bearing it safely. No affection is supposed to be shown, and yet by not sitting beside a particular person one can arouse jealousy.

According to one fisherman, the two factors that make life at sea difficult are the uncertainty about luck and "agitation." The advice given me constantly during the first weeks at sea was "be tranquil"; they feared "agitation," anxiety and defeatism. A true fisherman, especially a *pesca*, needs to give the appearance of being immune to danger. Toughness is the best means of scaring away the inner enemy.

At the same time, the mutual dependence among all crew members makes self-assertiveness a psychological necessity. I never heard a fisherman publicly admit any fault in himself in spite of the countless disputes. It would be an unnecessary and embarrassing gesture, for everyone knows that what is at stake is never authority or truth; it is easy to know who has made the slip, but it is necessary to maintain the appearance of being right in order to preserve a necessary measure of personal autonomy.

For similar reasons, public criticism is the norm on board: "To the bread, bread; and to the wine, wine" and "Let us see if we don't talk plain, since we are fishermen" are two expressions commonly heard when a complaint needs to be brought into the open. I myself was always admonished in public by the boatswain or a fisherman for any fault in my work. Complaints against the boatswain were also made publicly, and he was forced to justify his decisions, sometimes in a noisy argument with the accuser. Once when the *pesca* shouted at the boatswain, he responded by boldly shouting back in the presence of all the fishermen: "Go fuck yourself. You tell me to do the same, and we'll both have a go." Later, he explained his behaviour: "As he insulted me in public, I did the same to him in public. I need to keep my pride, otherwise I would lose the fishermen's respect."

The great sin is to get ploughed under (*achicarse*; literally, "to get smaller"). Swearing becomes the formula for exorcising dependence on natural and social factors. Each time a rolling sea forces the use of both hands just to keep standing, or the dish "runs away" from the table, or water invades the cabin through the ventilator, or nobody can hear a shout from the galley or the mess, a flow of sheer impotence explodes in, "Shit on God."

The idea of God among the fishermen is revealing of their overall psyche. Chatting about religious matters, I was told: "God and family are the same," or "God, although different, is the same thing as the family." The essential point is that for the fishermen, *both* God and family are otherworldly. For a fisherman in his late forties, "God is there to forgive. If we were perfect, God would not exist. His duty is to forgive everything wrong that we unconsciously do, for we are all human beings, and like a song repeats itself over and over, so we go on doing wrong unconsciously." The wife of a fisherman wrote to her husband, "I am a bit angry with you because you don't write me, you are slothful, but I will forgive you because, after all, I have to forgive you." Like a penitent after confessing his sins, a fisherman, coming out of the phone booth from which he had just called his wife, said: "What a relief! I am now satisfied; I am now ready to go back to the sea. I am a new man."

God becomes the protective idea that makes possible the general moral order and, at the same time, the ultimate Being responsible for all disorder: "I think of Him all the time. . . . Each time something goes wrong, you remember God and say 'Shit on God.' You don't say 'Shit on whores' or shit on something else but 'Shit on God.'" Indeed, the blasphemy is constantly heard on board. As for the family, it becomes the protective institution that promises constant emotional pleasure and is at the same time responsible for inspiring the sacrifice of life at sea. Both these sets of facts are included in the same logical/emotional structure that counterbalances seamen's psychological risk at sea.

Unlike the 'landlubber,' who may attach strong emotional projections to religious mythologies that are distinguishable from family identifications, the sentiment of the deep-sea fisherman towards his family becomes so distant that it is invested with the transcendence the landlubber projects on the religious order. The original family situation in itself is spatially, temporally and psychologically so distant that the emotions felt towards it may be akin to religious feelings and may even serve the same function. "Fishermen are like children," said one fisherman to me.

The distance or otherworldliness of God is important also in relation to the fishermen's thinking about luck. As Chapter 3 will show, luck, not God, is called upon to explain and mediate contradictions in natural causation and events. If the "prison" of the uncertain sea demands luck's help first of all, God, by contrast, stays at a distance—in the paradise of shore pleasures and family enjoyment.

"Being a fisherman" implies a lifetime occupation that, as the Newfoundland fishermen put it, "gets in your blood." Being a fisherman is not necessarily thought of (by the fishermen) in terms of an economic contract. It is not the contract with a shipowner, or the ownership of a small boat, that makes a man a fisherman; rather an individual *is* a fisherman, and insofar as he is a fisherman, he is hired to work at sea. "Even if I later worked in a factory, I would still consider myself a fisherman," said one of them to me.

Endurance of the physical and mental hardships at sea, the constant challenge of luck and risk, disdain for the restrained and the easy, deprivation of family—all these make a Terranova fisherman a secretly daring and detached person, proud of overcoming the humiliation inherent in an occupation which entails offering and risking his life. "The life of the sea leaves a mark" is a common saying among fishermen. His personal style is unmistakable: his movements are brusque and energetic, a knife hangs from his belt, he wears water dress and long rubber boots, his hands are swollen, he smells of fish. His virtues are many: courage, openness, resistance to pain, toughness, love for his family. The sense of risk, and an instinctive alertness to it, are ingrained. When he is back home sleeping with his wife and he wakes up startled, it is probably because he dreamt he was being shouted at in a manoeuvre. One fisherman, in a delirium after a stomach operation, was found with his hands in the air, apparently repairing a net.

The status of a fisherman is set off from that of an officer, engineer-oiler, cook and cookee. Just as engines define the engineer-oilers' occupation, the net defines a fisherman's. His territory is defined by the deck, where the net is let out, where the net is hauled back, where the net holds the precious fish, where the net rests, where the net is repaired. The fisherman is the one on board who has the sense of being a proletarian, who feels that he has no specialization, that he will always be exploited, and that he ultimately performs the "real" fishing work. (Nevertheless, if he has to shovel salt in the hold, he protests: "I am a fisherman and not a quarry worker.")

His identity card, his passport, his driver's licence, his membership cards, his right to legal assistance—all this is summed up in a little book called a *cartilla*, his permit to go to sea. During the time of the voyage, his *cartilla* belongs to the shipowner, who keeps it as a legal guarantee until the fisherman withdraws from his ship or until the owner sends it back to him as a sign that his services are no longer wanted. A fisherman who learns, just before sailing, that he is going to be paid at a rate lower than the one he had previously been informed of has only one recourse to save his dignity: to go to the shipowner's office and in a trembling voice ask for his *cartilla* so that he can return home, because "the ships are yours, but the *cartilla* is mine."

The psychological mortgage he pays ashore for his "being a fisherman" is vast. He has been dreaming of getting out of the prison of the sea for months, and yet after two or three weeks at home, he yearns to be back at sea. Ashore he has no work, no knowledge, no risk, no other world to which he can return. He may spend hours reading newspapers five months old. He has nothing to say to people ashore. All he has thought about for months is fish and home, luck and family. Emotional projections are replaced by reality. One fisherman, who had work opportunities on shore, admitted the possibility that he kept returning to sea to preserve the feeling for his family, "because otherwise its intensity could be lost." It seems that the imagined family, constructed during separation from the real one, had become an object of emotional attachment capable of competing with it.

At last, after supper on 8 January, the first lights of the port of Vigo could be seen in the distance, and the fishermen came on deck to see with their own eyes if it was really true. Each knew that soon he was going to see "them." "When I am approaching home, first of all I start trembling with fear. You never know what has happened. Once I brought a present for somebody who had died. Then suddenly it is the great happiness of my wife and children."

The movements of the ships were never as slow and solemn as they seemed when relatives could be seen standing on the harbour front—nearly five months of desire were making this moment intensely felt. Our faces seemed strange to one another as the world of the ship relinquished its hold on us and each made a solitary return to his own family, his own god. No expressions of group solidarity, such as singing, joking, discussing, or swearing, were allowed to profane the occasion. The sound of the ships' engines unfolded in our silence as we approached the land of return.

Notes

1. Although the words are *todo me perdura* ("all remains in me"), the fishermen sing *todo me tortura* ("all tortures me").

2. I have described (and therefore separated) cognitive relations in one chapter and affective relations in another for analytical purposes only, for it would be quite wrong to think of luck as an exclusively cognitive fact or home as a distinctly emotional one. One way of putting it is that the sea situation is thought of fundamentally in terms of luck and the shore situation in terms of family affection.

My information about the men's family life is gathered mostly from the conversations at sea and so reflects their idealizations of life at home. When the voyage was over, I stayed in the home port for ten days and spent another twelve days in four villages, visiting the fishermen's families at their invitation. However, apart from getting a general impression of their family lives, I cannot rely much on my observations, for I felt their interaction was more at a social than at a family level while I was with them.

3. It can be very disturbing when a young daughter does not recognize her own father in bed with her mother and cries, "Who is that man?" This actually happened to a man from our trawler.

4. Nevertheless, the fishermen are aware that their wives can feel deprived also, without their presence as husbands. One man repeatedly

reminded me of the speech given by the Minister of Fisheries, in which he praised "the heroism of fishermen's wives" above and beyond the sacrifices of the fishermen themselves.

5. It could be argued that, in Leach's basic cosmological dichotomies, the fisherman categorizes his wife as "asexual:clean:sinless," whereas a prostitute is categorized as "sexual:dirty:sinful" (cf. Leach 1976: 75).

6. I was informed that, compared with other voyages, the amount of 'extracurricular' cooking done on our voyage was "just nothing"—probably because of the galley's bad location.

7. I was an exception to this rule. The peculiar shipboard social context modifies the meaning of emotional manifestations; just as sex in port was different from sex at home, likewise anger on board was different from anger ashore. A good example of this is the way fishermen related to me; they accepted me as a companion and frequently showed me their esteem, but I was accepted rather as a companion living outside their world (i.e., I was not a fisherman) who had come fishing for reasons that were unclear. On the surface they would try to inculcate me with "being a fisherman," but if I said or did something they considered rude or seamanlike, some voice of censure would soon be heard: "You are becoming uneducated like a fisherman."

Therefore, my emotional reactions also had a different significance from theirs. For instance, the fact that my face looked solemn when waking up one morning in harbour upset three fishermen, who immediately asked what was wrong with me; after lunch they commented on it to me, so that I could deny that I was irritated. Fishermen generally do not worry about each other's moodiness. Similarly, my outburst of anger over a trivial matter provoked in them unusual conciliatory gestures towards me for two days. I was led to the conclusion that shipboard anger—which they had difficulties in attributing to me—needs to be understood within the shipboard system of social communication. As such, venting one's anger is a good means of creating and keeping fluent social relations, avoiding negligence in each one's role-fulfillment and the danger of hidden resentments.

8. Unlike the *pesca*, the captain normally does not need to reinforce his authority with an overbearing attitude, because he enjoys the advantage of being a career man and because his field of authority is not properly fishing but administration.

9. Partially, it was my peculiar position of belonging to the shipboard organization as a crew member, and at the same time being consi-

dered outside the shipboard cognitive and emotional orders, that made me the object of excessive vigilance on their part. Also, some competition took place between the officers and fishermen, particularly at the beginning of the voyage, as to which group I was going to associate myself with.

The *pareja* in harbour after one of the trawlers was damaged in a storm.

Splicing the broken cables after the trawl stuck fast on the bottom of the bank—a particularly profitless and, in winter weather, painful task to be performed on the open deck.

Right: The full net rises to the surface as the two wings of the trawl are rewound by the receiving ship's winch. (Photo by J. Beobide.)
Below: A view of the cables from deck as the net is hauled in. The cables pass through blocks and tackles on top of the bridge and at deck level.

Above: Hauling in the net. *Right:* A full net on deck; the fishermen empty it into the fish ponds through the flush hatch.

Above:
Processing fish on board.
Left:
A trawler's engine room.
(Photos by J. Beobide.)

A salter at work, salting each of the fish individually. (Photo by J. Beobide.)

Some difficulties of work on a trawler. (Photos by J. Beobide.)

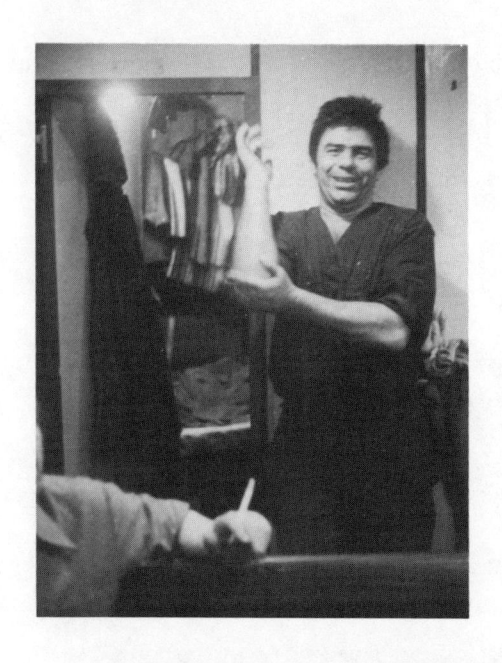

Above: The art of singing with a flourish; in the rear, the cramped living quarters.
Right: Expressive boozing. Sing the circle again!

CHAPTER 3

The Order of Luck

6.36311   It is a hypothesis that the sun will rise tomorrow: and this means that we do not *know* whether it will rise.

6.37   There is no compulsion making one thing happen because another has happened. The only necessity that exists is *logical* necessity.

6.371   The whole modern conception of the world is founded on the illusion that the so-called laws of nature are the explanations of natural phenomena.

6.372   Thus people today stop at the laws, treating them as something inviolable, just as God and Fate were treated in past ages. And in fact both are right and both wrong: though the view of the ancients is clearer insofar as they have a clear and acknowledged terminus, while the modern system tries to make it look as if *everything* were explained.

—Wittgenstein (1961: 143)

The Problem of Chance

Every Terranova fisherman must be ready to accept as a matter of course the extreme fluctuations of the catch and the absence of fish for one day, one week, or longer (see Appendix). On our voyage, for example, one day yielded more fish than the following fifteen days. A fisherman soon learns that the quantity of fish caught and his earnings (90 percent of which are based on the catch totals) depend on mere chance. Therefore, the relationship that a Terranova fisherman establishes with uncertain natural resources is a primary element of his occupational outlook.

A fisherman's perception of the nature of his occupation as a means of subsistence takes on the following 'beliefs':

1. The sea as supplier of the resource and the fisherman exploiting the resource live in close proximity, but the sea is not directly accessible. Furthermore, the sea is sensed as a constant danger.

2. Work is the means by which the fisherman approaches the sea and gains access to the resources; however, work in itself cannot guarantee a cause-and-effect relationship.

3. Between the worker and the aim of his work (fish), there is a gap that cannot be bridged by human effort alone; the successful bridging of this gap is understood to depend on chance—or the uncontrollable natural order. The fact that a cause-and-effect relationship cannot be applied to the fishing mode of production brings about a peculiar distance between the fisherman and the sea, since no working disposition, no concrete method, no known technique can provide success "until the right time comes."

4. Because the output resulting from the combination of work and resources is unknown and uncontrollable, the probability that the combination will occur is categorized as a new element, whose presence is logically necessary to bridge the gap between work and output. This new element is conceptualized as luck.

5. Since the fisherman, by his action, provokes the concurrence of two independent factors (work and fish), he becomes the mediator between the two otherwise unbridgeable realities by means of luck, a variable that belongs to neither the natural nor human order.

The natural order appears to a fisherman as irregularity and arbitrariness; his problem is how to order the disorder of the natural resources. The facts upon which the fisherman bases his ordering represent his basic economic and emotional needs.

Nevertheless, the peculiarity of his thinking arises from the occupational necessity of continuously bridging the gap between the human and natural orders, between work and catch. The matching of these two dimensions of reality is rendered verbally and conceptually workable by the term "luck."

The different levels of reality are interchangeable symbolically: natural order:fish::economic order:money::logical order: luck. Because of its connection with the above symbols, fish-processing, or more generally, "having work," becomes the desired occupational situation instead of being just a duty.

Although fish, money and luck are, roughly speaking, interchangeable, the prominence of luck at the time of fishing arises from its being the medium through which the other two orders are made possible. Where the natural order is taken as existing, and the economic order is a subsequent reward, the immediate aim of the fisherman at sea is the collaboration of natural and technical conditions. Luck is the nominalization of the logical space, or area of possibilities, wherein all the chance variations take place, and it tends to become reified as a cosmological entity.

Some definitions of luck, as it is experienced by fishermen, are (the categorizations are mine):

Cosmological: Luck is that state of affairs that is present when natural resources become available to human action.

Logical: Luck is that state of affairs ensuring that, in the logical space, fishing possibilities are actual or virtual realities.

Philosophical: Luck is that state of affairs the arbitrary causation of which governs the world in an uncontrollable way.

Psychological: Luck is that state of affairs in which human expectations arise and are regulated.

Economic: Luck is that state of affairs that makes possible economic profits, through the combination of the natural and technical orders.

Affective: Luck is that state of affairs that, with economic profits, allows family life.
Social: Luck is that state of affairs that legitimizes the institutional life on board a *pareja* trawler.

Fishermen's Conception of Luck

How is the nature of luck expressed by fishermen? *Tener suerte*, "to have luck," in its optative-interrogative form of "let us see whether we have luck," was the expression voiced countless times and even more often mentally invoked by all of us on board. The expression shows that luck is imagined as an entity that can be possessed. Since luck is the condition for the conjunction of economic and cosmological orderings, it is primarily a certain 'state of affairs' that is enclosed within a concrete spatio-temporal sequence; somehow it has to *happen*, be present at a certain place and time, become a factor at the disposition of one fisherman or another. Therefore, luck is originally understood by fishermen in terms of the continuum absence-presence, and the term "luck" is applied to the natural irregularity of the coming of fish.

Once luck becomes thought of in quantitative terms ("a bit of luck," "a lot of luck," "very little luck," "no luck"), positive and negative qualities are attached to it as well: luck is "good" when the minimal expectations have been realized; luck is "bad" when the minimal expectations have not been realized. Negative labelling becomes necessary when luck is not only absent but becomes visible through an actual negative reality, such as engine trouble or a personal accident. Nevertheless, fishermen distinguish between these negative realities and "not having luck," since "a mechanical fault can be repaired by the engineers," and "a personal accident could be caused by carelessness."

The difference between "bad luck" and "no luck" lies in being able to attribute a cause to the former, which is of natural (sea, weather), technical (engines, trawl) or human (illness, carelessness) origin and ultimately subject to correction; "no luck," on the other hand, cannot be blamed on any known cause. A forced visit to harbour for repairs or for medical treatment summarizes the "bad luck" of the above cases. But bad weather at sea—"that is not a matter of luck, that is just bad weather. You are not responsible for it, and everybody knows that it has to come and pass away." No luck is more painful because you cannot explain why it is, whereas you know that bad luck can be corrected or that carelessness has occurred. To explain bad luck, a natural or technical fault can be invoked, but with no luck there is no explanation or justification possible.

Luck on Our Voyage

What follows is a brief history of our voyage from the viewpoint of the dependence on luck. Before we left Spain on 21 August 1976 the hope of having a successful voyage was constantly present in our conversations. "If we have a bit of luck we shall be back home by Christmas," was the statement most often heard, summarizing certain associated desires: that no engine trouble or personal loss would make a normal trip impossible, or that we would make a sufficiently good catch in time to return home for Christmas, with all its emotional implications.

As a group we were perfectly aware of the constraints of the institutional structure and the ecological circumstances. Social relations on board would be a very important factor for the well-being of the crew. Our catches would depend on the *pesca*'s expertise. The men had to be prepared to endure for days the hardship of uninterrupted work and bad weather conditions; we knew that just one member was enough to agitate the whole crew should he refuse to work or, even worse, suffer a mental breakdown.

In any case, these were all factors somehow "under our control": the expertise of the *pesca* was not questioned; there would be some way to handle bad social relations; the fishermen's disposition to work was quite clear; total incompetence or illness of a member could be resolved by sending him home and substituting another member.

We were more concerned with what we could not control and with what was going to decide the success or disaster of the voyage: the availability of fish in the banks we were going to work. Gradually our emotional ties with relatives, friends and home were replaced by a total uncertainty about returning. Crew solidarity was based mainly on that uncertainty and the group's direct relation to fishing possibilities. In this sense, the mental systematization of those possibilities and the constant reliance on that system to legitimize our institutional 'abnormality' was central to understanding life on board. At the logical level, the possibility of not catching anything was compensated for by keeping in mind the whole range of possibilities; likewise, emotionally, the actual fear provoked by that uncertainty needed to be compensated for by faith in those possibilities. The boundaries of our social reality were set by the uncertain availability of the natural resource we pursued. Although money, work, isolation and social relations were also obvious factors that bound us, it was the actual risk and cognitive dependence that typified our situation. We were defined by what we could not control.

After the first twenty days of fishing off Greenland, we were asking ourselves how well we had done. The *pareja* had caught about one hundred tons of fish. This figure gave our hopes direction as far as estimating how large a catch to expect on the entire voyage; roughly, we could catch one hundred tons in fifteen days. At this rate, if our luck held, we could catch a total of seven hundred tons before Christmas, which makes a "very good" voyage. However, by no means did we give up expecting a larger catch. Everybody knew that the best fishing month was going to be November on the bank of St. Pierre, for so it had been in former years with our *pesca*. And I heard the captain say several times: "Once September and October are over, with a bit of fish, we are saved." In reality, we depended on the game of chance, in which luck, by its magic, would correct at any moment the imbalance in actual catches according to our expectations as the trip progressed.

On the way to St. John's, we all made up our minds about our catches and shared an estimate. The beginning had been fine. In the test of Greenland, what mattered more than the catch itself was that future chances were confirmed. In the least likely fishing place and time, we had adjusted to a minimum expectation of seven hundred tons for the voyage, and still more could be anticipated. My bet with a salter was that we would get eight hundred tons by Christmas.

Needless to say, this mental settling-up was important for all of us when a mechanical fault disrupted the fishing after only twenty days at sea. This frame of mind was the protection we needed against the frustration and fear of not knowing how long engine problems would keep us in harbour. An elementary calculation would have made it clear that the earnings of the first month, based on the one hundred tons of fish caught, were markedly insufficient. Nevertheless, that was not the way we looked at the issue. All our economic compromises had been translated into cognitive schemes, and they indicated that our chances were good after the first twenty days of fishing.

On 25 September we left St. John's, and twelve hours later the net was dragging. During the following week we caught 120 tons of very good fish in just seventy-nine hours! That, and nothing else, was fishing. That was luck.

But again we ran into bad luck and had to accept the fisherman's lot. Just one week after we left St. John's, the cookee in the companion trawler fell into a diabetic coma. I was ordered to the bridge to call St. John's and contact the doctor at the Spanish Seamen's Centre, who ordered an immediate return to port, feeling confident that the man could be saved. The chief engineer was ordered to proceed full speed ahead to cover the eighteen hours that separated us from port. There we were, fifty-two men leaving behind our marvellous catches to take to port a crew member whose survival was uncertain. We reached harbour in time and the crewman did survive.

On the morning of 6 October we were back sailing, and by midnight we had seven tons of fish on board. Next midday the companion trawler caught twelve tons. We had been abandoned by luck for three days and were most uncertain about its still being where we left it. During the following days we fished very well (see Appendix, p. 111).

On 19 October a tremendous storm came up and the companion trawler was dangerously damaged. The surf swept over the bridge, broke two windows and damaged the radars, automatic steering and radio equipment; the water flooded the fishermen's cabins too. The crew found themselves unable to control the ship; since it was not possible to turn into the storm, the waves started hitting the trawler sideways and heeling her over dangerously. For three long hours of anxiety, they lost all contact with us and they feared the worst. During all this time our crew was completely unaware of their critical situation, for our *pesca* had the radio which was used for communication between the two trawlers switched off during all those hours, making it impossible for the damaged trawler to get in touch with us. It was only when the helmsman replaced the *pesca* on the bridge and turned on the radio that the whole episode became known to us.

Once in port, the crew of the damaged trawler told us about the terrible hours during which they believed they were going to sink. But by then it was already a matter of fact—a frightening event to be told, one more product of the sea's sheer, blind arbitrariness, out of man's control—the kind of event that gives rise to fishermen's fatalism: "What must be, will be." I did not hear one fisherman wondering whether the strength of the storm could have been anticipated by radio weather forecasts so that the *pareja* would have had time to move to the safety of St. John's harbour, which was only eighty miles distant. Neither did anybody point to the fact that had our *pesca* (otherwise an extremely watchful man) not turned off the radio, the other trawler's crew would have been greatly relieved by the presence of our trawler by their side. It would have been rather ludicrous for the fishermen to blame anybody for what happened, for bad luck was behind it all.

After all, perhaps this was part of learning what "being a fisherman" was like and how irrelevant 'normal' social interactions and mechanical work could be when everything depended on uncontrollable factors. Not knowing what to expect and lack of order were normal conditions on board our *pareja*.

On 18 October we caught 26 tons of fish. But the following fifteen days (five of them in harbour, ten at sea) yielded only 25 tons, less than on that previous single day. On 1 November, another day without any fish, the *pesca*'s anxiety became obvious. "When you are not catching, your morale is down in your feet," he said to me while I served him lunch, which he did not eat because he was not hungry. "Other *parejas* are fishing well on this same bank, but we don't have the luck. This will pass, my God," he added. The next day, we still did not get any fish. There was no excuse for not catching in that month and on that bank. The *pesca* had no appetite the following day, and for the first time I heard fishermen mildly criticizing a decision he had made. Each of the other *parejas* had caught, during the last few days, 40 to 50 tons—while we caught nothing. The week we fished 120 tons we all took for granted that our trawler's fishing capacity and our *pesca*'s expertise were the best in the whole Terranova fleet. Now we were forced to abandon that assumption. The helmsman, very concerned, remarked to me: "At sea, when things start going wrong, it is a fuck-up." Next day, the helmsman pointed out to me a *pareja* not more than two miles away: "Look, yesterday that *pareja* caught 20 tons. It is just luck."

However, on the night of 3 November our companion trawler caught four tons, and the next morning, five tons. The whole picture changed, along with our expectations. Early that morning the captain confidently reassured me (and himself) that luck was changing: "You see, yesterday we had four tons"—which I understood as "We are again catching fish, and are saved."

In the following twelve days we caught two hundred tons. But on 17 November we headed for St. Pierre without knowing the reason. Later we learned that the *pesca* of another *pareja* (who was a brother of our *pesca*) was having an argument with the Spanish chaplain at St. Pierre who had criticized over the radio the *pesca*'s treatment of the fishermen. The *pesca* in question had called other *parejas* to support him in the dispute.

We had been forced into harbour the first time because of engine trouble, the second time because of one fisherman's diabetic coma, the third time because of storm damage, and the fourth because of a *pesca*'s anger at a chaplain's attempts to champion fishermen's rights. Together, the four situations provide a good sample of the untoward circumstances affecting the Terranova fishermen's work.

On 21 November we were sailing again (see Appendix, p. 112). From 23 November to 2 December the fishermen worked an average of sixteen hours per day for ten days, catching a total of 320 tons. We were having luck. I heard the captain repeat three times on 25 November: "What has to happen, has to happen." It was all a gratuitous gift merited by our challenging luck, the reward for so much physical and psychological risk.

When embarking on the challenge of this particular voyage, we could not be sure of the time it would take to fill the hold—time being one more consequence of success or failure. Nevertheless, all our expectations were directed to a voyage sufficiently successful so that we would be allowed to return home by Christmas. At the beginning of December, the voyage was already won and there was no sense in prolonging the battle.

On 9 December I heard a veteran fisherman saying something that just two weeks before would have sounded blasphemous: "I would sign right now for not one single fish more to come." Likewise, when I asked about the number of tons caught, I was told that "now it's better if we don't get any fish, for if we are fishing well they are going to order us to continue here during Christmas, but if we don't catch any fish from now on, they will send us home." Suddenly we were no longer praying for luck and work.

But the *pareja* caught about fifty tons on 12 and 13 December. We were enjoying luck once again, in spite of our turning our backs on it. However, this luck had a clearly different quality. Until then, luck had been defined basically in economic terms, and indirectly by the affective reward of making possible the return; now, in the middle of December, luck was defined primarily in terms of facilitating the end of the voyage and only secondarily by the economic profits.

On the night of 19 December we had a good haul of eight tons, but it was not a cause for rejoicing. The boatswain commented, "I would leave it all and go to sleep." What he meant was that the only possible contentment, at that time, was emotional; since luck, in terms of economics, could not help us in reaching our more immediate goal, it was not worthy of being enjoyed. We had definitely left behind the particular mental process that had ordered our social and psychological life up to that point. With regard to shipboard routine, December passed much the same as the other months, but how different the work had been in September! Only cognitive facts could explain the difference, for the work as such was secondary, compared with the emotional need or the arbitrariness of luck. In the end, our voyage was a very successful one; we caught a lot of fish, no accidents occurred, the social relations were excellent. What was hard to appreciate was the extent to which our final success had been set by our initial uncertainty and fear.

The Ambivalence of Luck

Whether it is regarded as possibility or actuality, cosmology or psychology, fiction or reality, luck is the key concept around which all the fishermen's expectations are centred. In a way, all the rest is a matter of previous assumption: trawlers, technology, skill, work, and even the existence of fish. It is the connection between the natural and human orders that is a question mark; the conditions ordering this connection are therefore the main cognitive problem.

The relationship of fishermen to luck displays some asymmetry. First of all, there is no direct cause-and-effect relationship between human powers and luck. Since luck in itself is totally gratuitous, as daily variations in catch show, all that can be done remains in the stage of preparation. In general, the features of the relationship between the fisherman and his source of livelihood that were analysed earlier are here transposed into the relationship between the fisherman and luck.

If, instead of cause-and-effect, we adopt the form of subject-object, then luck becomes the not-directly-reachable and impersonal object for the subject-fisherman. The consequence of luck being considered an arbitrary effect is the tendency in fishermen to believe in arbitrary causes. The inability to influence luck by human means creates in the fisherman a fatalistic disposition; since any calculation has to end with the hope "If we have a bit of luck," everything is placed at the mercy of luck. Nobody has a right to have luck. One owns it only gratuitously and temporarily; no protest or hostility can be directed against it. The only way a man has access to luck is through hope, expectation, belief.

Although beyond human control, luck provokes a peculiar type of responsibility in men, because luck is a state of affairs that makes possibilities become actualities. It is obvious that you are not responsible for not having luck when you are contributing as much as you can; at the same time, it seems obvious that if the *pareja* that is two miles away has a good catch while you have no catch at all, you are somehow responsible for not provoking the state of affairs that would make the catching possibility become an actuality. In other words, because logically there are unlimited fishing spots but only one that can be chosen at a time, up to the time of making the decision for the fishing spot, you are not responsible for it; but in case it turns out that your decision was wrong, then you are responsible for it afterwards, since you could have chosen other fishing places. Thus, a fisherman, through the mediation of the *pesca*, is responsible for the variations in luck in a way that he is not responsible for bad weather conditions.

Responsibility gives ground to guilt, in that when luck is absent the 'fault' has to be somehow discovered. "If only I knew where the fault was!" was the *pesca*'s exclamation during a period of no catches. On these occasions, two means of dealing with the frustration were put into practice. One was technical: the *pesca*, the sole person responsible for the fishing strategy, ordered the seven tons of tackle to be examined inch by inch. "If fish were coming the trawl would be okay, but since they are not . . . ," one fisherman explained to me. The other means was verbal exorcism of suspected witchcraft. For example, in this case, the chaplain in St. John's was blamed for the absence of fish: "It's his fault for saying that we could catch ten tons per day and leave for Spain by 18 December." Fishermen were perfectly aware, of course, that the absence of fish was due neither to witchcraft nor to faulty tackle but simply to "no luck." Nevertheless, group solidarity required this ritual behaviour. We did not have luck, but there had to be some way of expressing our unity and collective readiness for its return; the significant thing was the rite itself, even though we knew that there were no means of bringing about a change in the arbitrary causation of luck.

Thus the ordering process of luck, on the one hand, brings personal responsibility to bear where utmost arbitrariness rules; on the other hand, luck ensures that fishermen are less responsible for their lack of success. Instead of blaming the absence of industry-related marine research, lack of technological development, or even a miscalculation on the part of the *pesca*, they attribute responsibility to a cosmological entity.

Luck and the Daily Catch

Luck structures the meaning fishermen give to the daily catch. In economic terms a haul of ten tons of fish means about $50 in earnings per crewman; however, in relation to the thousand tons that are needed to fill up the *pareja*, the significance of ten tons lies not in the number as such, but rather in the sense of order it creates in the fishermen's expectations. The convictions that "There is fish," "We are going to have a good voyage," "We are going to be home by Christmas," "We have luck" are the primary messages conveyed by the daily catches. As with the totemic man, for whom "the idea of totem [is] cardinal . . . [and who] is under a necessity to place everything else that he knows in relation to it" (Durkheim and Mauss 1963: 82), the fisherman needs to relate everything to luck, because it is the kernel of his thinking.

At the beginning of the voyage, we had fifteen weeks to fill up the *pareja*, or at least to round off the voyage to a point at which we would be allowed to go home by Christmas. The all-pervading secret game started in our minds: roughly, we had 100 days to catch 1,000 tons; for "things to go well," the *pareja* needed to catch an average of ten tons per day. (The fishermen taught me this calculation the first day I joined them in Vigo.) Later on, I heard the captain correcting the above estimate: "I would be satisfied with eight tons per day." However, we did not have to bind ourselves unconditionally to that possibility. One thousand tons in less than four months would constitute an extraordinary voyage; 900 tons would also be an excellent voyage, and even 800 tons was a real success—a figure anybody on board would "sign right now." Seven hundred tons was still a very good voyage, and 600 tons would not be a failure.

In any case, there was an important factor that was going to excuse an unsuccessful result and protect us from failure. This was the first time that our trawlers were going to fish in Terranova (they had fished for other species in Africa), and it was our job to test their efficiency. Thus, the technological uncertainty was converted into a defence in case of failure; after all, "we were just going to try out the *pareja* in the period before Christmas." But we would not talk about this defence since the challenge lay in gambling with the number of tons—1,000, 900, 800, 700—that might be caught before Christmas. It was only at the end of the voyage, when failure was no longer a possibility, that this fact was brought up on several occasions. The *pesca* confessed in December that the shipowner had wished him "to have a bit of luck, catch something, and return by Christmas," and he complained about the shipowner's change of attitude when the voyage proved successful in terms of catches (for in the end, we were not allowed home for Christmas). The boatswain too declared that the *pesca* had assured him before leaving Spain that if we caught 600 to 700 tons, we would return by Christmas.

The ordering or disordering effects of the catches depend on their relationship to luck; for example, two days without a catch have the same economic significance regardless of cause, but the psychological implications are quite different, depending on whether the cause is known or unknown. Whereas a day of 'lying to' because of adverse weather conditions means a passive acceptance, an unsuccessful day of dragging is positively a failure in getting luck; in the first case the cause is well known, in the second case it is unknown. Likewise, a week of repairs in harbour and a week of no catches have the same result in terms of economics, but they have radically different connotations.

As a simple illustrative model, let us suppose that the expectation for a given month is 150 tons and that the catches follow four patterns whose final outcome reaches the expected figure, but in different weeks of the month:

Pattern	First Week	Second Week	Third Week	Fourth Week	Total
a	0	50	50	50	150 tons
b	50	50	50	0	150 tons
c	50	50	0	50	150 tons
d	50	0	50	50	150 tons

Although the expected net catch was achieved in all cases, it is easily appreciated how the frame of expectations at the end of the month would be quite different in each pattern. A fisherman's mind is constantly abstracting models of this kind from the actual catches for future projections on the basis of different time divisions.

According to probability calculus, the more information a statement contains, the greater the number of ways in which it may turn out to be false. In their way, fishermen make constant use of the principle of higher informative content, and therefore lower probability, since luck is in inverse relationship to probability— that is, the lower the probability of its happening, the greater the luck; the greater the probability, the lower the luck. This was the case on 7 October, when our trawler got "only" three and a half tons, an amount that at the beginning of September was considered definitely good; or on 29 October, when our trawler got "only" six tons and moved a hundred miles in hopes of better catches. In normal conditions six tons of fish make an excellent cast, but at the end of October, on St. Pierre Bank and after a week of repairs, the informative content of luck was projected towards huge casts of fifteen to twenty tons. Fishing becomes a matter of luck simply because there is always the possibility of its not yielding good results. By contrast, in merchant ships the economic or working possibilities need not be predicted with the same urgency, and the focus on luck, although present, is not central in the daily orientation to work.

Fishermen are well aware that luck is ultimately a fiction of their own. Nevertheless, it is for them the best available explanation of the contrast between actual events and anticipated ones. Fundamentally, luck for a fisherman is his way of thinking, since all the symbolic patterns he constructs have the hidden purpose of provoking, so to speak, a regular output or "program" of luck (see Geertz 1973).[1] For a fisherman, both the set of processes that acts as a program, and the programmed set, are based on the assumption of luck; that is, his thinking goes from past luck to future luck, establishing a congruence where all seems irregularity and making use of that irregularity to manipulate the programs experimentally.

What we learn then from the fisherman's perception of his own experience is that thought deals primarily with the limits of its own knowledge, for luck at the conceptual level means "arbitrary causation," "beyond understanding." Another lesson is the importance of anticipation in thought processes. For Cree hunters, "divination fills in gaps in knowledge which cannot be learned from the environment" and "is not a substitute for environmental data-gathering, but a parallel process which is of a symbolic order" (Tanner 1979: 134). Similarly, fishermen's thinking in terms of luck revolves around a continuous prediction of the availability of a natural resource.

When luck is regarded as a cosmological entity by the fishermen, then metaphysics or superstition appears in their thinking.[2] Dependence on luck immersed us, as a crew, in a mental state that might be called a magical attitude on those few occasions when luck was felt to be an active and purposeful agent, rather than a passive effect of arbitrary causation. The time when we came closest to this situation was at the beginning of November, after five days of repairs in harbour and ten days without a catch at sea, during a time when expectations were highest. The incident occasioning it was my report to the bridge of a stormy weather forecast, which I had heard on the radio. But as all Spanish weather forecasts for Terranova are held to be inaccurate, my report became a cause of anger and scorn. That same evening, when I was accused by the chief engineer of wanting to bring bad luck to the *pareja*, I jokingly replied that I wished we would have a couple of hours of real storm. To my surprise, my reply caused the *pesca* (a modern man who despises superstititions) to threaten me with being sent back to Spain at the first opportunity. I would be "paid for the whole voyage"—the formula for sending home somebody who deserves respect but is not wanted on the ship. The forecast proved to be right the next day.

I was playing a very dangerous game: first, I did not seem to be concerned about the precarious situation on board after fifteen days without a catch; second, I had dared to mention the desire for bad weather. What else but desire had been our single means of dealing with frustration all those days? And now I was jokingly turning it against the crew's interests. In that situation, whatever we had on our minds, and even more, its verbalization, became particularly significant.

Luck and the Ritual of Fishing

If luck, for its otherworldly action, needs a temple, the ship is just that: a liminal and exorcised place where, although fishermen will say "We don't believe in them," verbal taboos are still observed. There must be no umbrellas or broken mirrors, and when a crew member took a cat aboard, I heard the captain asking the *pesca* whether a cat was permitted. Adding to the unearthly quality of life aboard ship is the pervasiveness of a marine vocabulary, distinct from the language used on land. For example, floor, room, bed, wall, window, rope, cable become deck, berth, bunk, bulkhead, porthole, line, hawser, respectively. The points of orientation refer to the four sides of the ship: there is no north, south, east, west, but bow, stern, starboard, portside.

If the ritual of luck requires prayer, then the continuous dragging of the net day and night may be assumed to fulfill this end. Most of all, if the ritual requires a sacrifice, the fishermen are there to offer their work and their lives in order to receive the gift of fish. Since fish and fish-processing mean money, and imply that luck was present once more, fishermen end up associating luck with work, risk and physical exhaustion. Day or night, Sunday or Monday, weekday or holiday, there is no greater gift for a Terranova fisherman than a good haul of ten to fifteen tons. Physical work is no longer a punishment, but a sign of luck. The real punishment is the constant threat to the order of expectations. Present penance becomes a guarantee for the happiness of the fishermen's future life ashore with the family.

The absence of fish is also an essential part of the sacrifice. The ultimate cause of it is to be found not in the natural resource (diminishing stocks of fish, variations in fish migratory movements) or in human action (a wrong decision, faulty information), but in something much more mysterious and familiar: no luck. Although fishermen are quite aware of technological improvements and the diminution of fish stocks, luck is the idea according to which they have ordered their thinking for a long time, and only the belief in its arbitrary causation can supply the daily energy to persevere with the ritual of fishing.

The Pesca and the Ritual of Fishing

The *pesca* enjoys the sacred immunity of being the mediator between the uncontrollable forces of luck and fishing. His decisions regarding the fishing operations were almost never evaluated by the crew as being right or wrong. Because of the charismatic enhancement of this mediation, it can be said that any fisherman believes that his *pesca* is "one of the best"; at least it was with ours, and with the *pescas* of all the *parejas* I visited. (I have never heard a fisherman denouncing his *pesca* as inefficient.) Since a *pesca*'s expertise is a necessary condition for the working of luck, the fishermen not only assume that his optimum performance is ensured, but they themselves are bound to him. Ultimately, then, the very nature of power at sea depends on luck.

This does not mean that no one ever complains about his *pesca*. On the contrary, he is frequently labelled "dog," "coyote," "slave trader" and other such derogatory terms. However, these terms indicate strength as well, and my impression is that a fisherman's image of his *pesca* includes toughness—enough to be immune to fear and social chaos on board. In general, any protest against the *pesca* is directed at the level of social relations or excessive demands on the fishermen; his expertise and decision-making are hardly ever questioned.

For a *pesca*, good catches mean an enormous income but, more important, they sustain his reputation as a skilled *pesca* in competition with others. He is personally responsible for the catches: if luck helps and the catches are good, his reputation remains intact; if he has no luck and few catches, he assumes the entire responsibility for failure. A week without catches is enough to "eat the guts" out of a *pesca* with worry.

One consequence of his position, which can lead to dangerous decisions, is the need to make use of the maximum working time when luck is with him. In practical terms this means that he must ask the fishermen to work savage hours in times of good catches (every fisherman has records of fifty to sixty hours of continuous work), or in stormy weather, to risk their lives performing deck manoeuvres in order to continue the dragging. The *pesca*'s aim is to get the most profit from an operation no matter what the weather conditions, since just one afternoon of dragging can mean four or five tons of fish; his share of this is about $300—a sum that could easily be doubled with a proportionate increase in catch.

On the other hand, a *pesca* faces the problem of status reinforcement, since everybody on board recognizes that he is essentially just "one more fisherman." In contrast to the captain who has done major nautical studies, or even to the engineers who have a profession, the *pesca* has no formal training. His knowledge comes with years of experience as a fisherman. Being tough, daring, uninhibited, provoking, blasphemous, indifferent to fatigue or fear—these qualities partly fulfill the function of reinforcing the *pesca*'s peculiar status of charismatic fisherman whose only claim to fame is mediator of luck.

Any analysis of the relationship between *pesca* and fishermen should take into account that, unlike the boss-worker relationship in a factory or the manager-secretary relationship in an office, the situation is such that everyone depends on luck, and everyone is away from his family, living instead in an institutionally forced association. Sometimes one or all of these factors put the *pesca* and the fishermen in the same position. For example, one consequence of their joint dependence on luck is not only that fishermen uncritically accept the *pesca*'s decisions, but also that they internalize his duty to maximize a good fishing opportunity even though it might cause them physical exhaustion for days. Once, during a period of non-stop work, I purposefully started attacking the *pesca*'s behaviour before three fishermen, arguing that his good treatment of us was a trap to make us work more without arousing our protests. My words must have sounded rebellious, for the fishermen were clearly embarrassed and pointed out: "We don't always have fish and when we do, we have to make the most of it." They declared that "as far as the shipowner is concerned, they [the *pescas*] are all the same, but in the way they treat us, *pescas* are as different [from one another] as day and night."

This same assumption of maximum work exploitation, which was accepted by the fishermen, was responsible for the fact that they considered it a sign of the *pesca*'s unexpected humanity when, after fifty-seven hours of heavy and nearly uninterrupted work between Tuesday midday and Friday night, he allowed them two hours of sleep before continuing to work for another fifty-six hours in the next three days. "There you have a sign of his fairness," I was assured; "see if some other *pesca* would give you two hours of rest, with fish in the park."

Ultimately, much about the *pesca*'s status depends on the way the fishermen view their relations to luck. For the chance of luck to be the best possible, the fishermen must first completely believe in it; in order for fish to be considered a gift, the arbitrariness of luck must be acknowledged. Similarly, fishermen tend to regard the *pesca*'s efficiency largely as a gift, a charisma, a safety guarantee. As with luck, their uncritical attitude of, submissiveness to, and faith in their *pesca* are absolute conditions for the symbolic and actual situations to correspond in the minds of every member of the *pareja*. A number of times—for example, when the net became entangled—I pointed out to the fishermen that the *pesca* was responsible for the trouble. Their reaction was a mixture of surprise, disbelief and scorn. Of course, they knew that if the *pesca* had not ordered dragging in that area, the net would not have become tangled. Yet what really mattered was not the course the *pesca* had set, but whether luck was with them. In other words, the decision in itself is not responsible; rather, it is the failure of nature to collaborate.

Structurally, the tendency is to personalize the *pesca*'s power on the basis that he is the only person responsible for the fishing strategy. Besides, as manager, the *pesca* makes full use of the fishermen's assumption that experience and cleverness do matter, and that it is the *pesca* who is uniquely endowed with these qualities. An example of this is our *pesca*'s reprimand of the companion trawler's chief engineer because he had shifted to the stern tank 15,000 litres of petrol, when the *pesca* had permitted him to shift only 12,000 litres: even a chief engineer needs the permission of the *pesca*, who has no engineering knowledge, to do something about problems of the ship's balance. The *pesca* muttered several times, "At sea mathematics do not count."

What are the distinguishing qualities of a *pesca*? From what I gathered from our *pesca*, the learning gleaned from years of working with expert *pescas* as a fisherman helps promote a likely career as *pesca*.[3] Knowledge of the best fishing spots, which are usually situated in the corners that the continental shelf forms against the deep sea, where the fish remain protected from the tidal currents, is imperative, as is knowledge of how to construct the net. But above all, a *pesca* must have the capacity for complete concentration on fishing. According to one captain, "That is what we mean when we say of some *pescas*, 'He is a fisherman.' Take me as an example. I know more about the net than any *pesca* in Terranova, except perhaps one, but I am not what is called a fisherman." When I asked if the relative capacity for concentration was noticeable in catch totals, his answer was: "Oh yes, they catch much more than I, because I don't have my mind focused on fishing twenty-four hours a day." Luck rewards the seaman to the degree the seaman believes in, and waits for, luck.

On this same matter of concentration, I once heard our *pesca* commenting on his need to shout continuously at a second *pesca* he once worked with "because he was not attentive," whereas to the present second *pesca* he never had to say anything, "because he is very attentive." In sum, to the fishermen's virtues of skill, courage and endurance of physical fatigue, the *pesca* (the archetypical fisherman) brings the virtue of attentiveness. By his mental capacity to focus on nothing else but fishing, to the point of obsession, the *pesca* negotiates, on behalf of the *pareja*, the ultimate dependence on luck.

The most frequent conflict between a *pesca* and a captain, according to our cook, is caused by the captain's supposed negligence in his night dragging. This was clearly the problem on our trawler when the *pesca* complained about the captain's novel-reading in the mornings, "and then he sleeps everywhere." The captain, after a full night's work on the bridge, used to read for one or two hours while having breakfast—his leisure time for the whole day. As far at the *pesca* was concerned, those two hours of frivolous reading broke the concentration on fishing and were reflected in his incomplete attentiveness to the night dragging. At the end of November the situation between them worsened, and the *pesca* started waking up the captain at suppertime more and more brusquely.

The shipowner plays no part in the ritual of fishing. Once at sea, the fisherman freely agrees to the working conditions laid down by the shipowner on shore and accepts the challenge of luck. When there is no fish for a day or a week, the fisherman does not blame his working contract, but the absence of luck. After all, who wants to have good catches more than the shipowner himself? The fisherman knows in his bones that the shipowner robs him, but that is always "after" the voyage is over, at the time of payment. The shipowner has nothing to do with the fisherman's not being lucky at sea. It is this kind of relationship with luck which makes it very difficult for the fisherman to call into question the traditional power arrangements as we have described them. This indicates that the ideology of luck has a much shorter scope and is of a different nature for the shipowner than for the fishermen.

Luck and Fatalism among Fishermen

Much of the implicit communication among the crew members springs from their sharing the same environmental-conceptual circumstances. Luck as a regulative concept creates a system which is accepted by everybody on board and is the basis of a strong occupational bond. Once, when there were no catches and I remarked on the seriousness of the fishermen during the dragging, the *pesca* accused me of laughing at them. The dependence on luck demands a certain emotional attitude that seems incompatible with an observant one. Since motives are meaningful with reference to ends, it is the conceptual order which provides those ends and the "liabilities to perform particular classes of acts or have particular classes of feeling" (Geertz 1973: 97). Luck offers the framework in which the economic motivations are turned into acts of communication. Through the patterning of luck and the emotional involvement it requires, the fisherman becomes aware of the demands of fishing on himself and the necessity for crew solidarity.

Another important point about the 'working' of luck is its formulaic aspect. Luck in fishing at a certain place and time is itself evidence of the correct formula, and everything must be done to avoid changes or breaks in this spatial-temporal frame. This is why the sense of loss was so poignant each time we were forced to interrupt a good fishing session and head for harbour. When we took up the voyage again we felt as if we were starting from the beginning. Once luck had favoured a particular spatial-temporal sequence, abandoning it for a few days was clearly to abandon luck and to have to wait for it again "from nothing." Likewise, when the *pesca* exclaimed in October, "I wish this month to end at last," luck had become identified with a certain month in a negative way.

It is the fishing itself that provides ground for the conceptual reification of luck. On the one hand, certain waters at certain periods (for instance, the bank at St. Pierre in November) are more bountiful than others, therefore creating an intrinsic relationship between the space/time and the catches; on the other hand, any fishing is chancy, and luck has to be predicated in advance, since the relationship is never intrinsic but symbolic (real only in the logical space). Thus luck offers the matrix wherein both kinds of predications are bridged: fishing exists as possibility before its occurrence, thanks to the order generated by the concept of luck; once fishing becomes a reality in catches, then luck (that was before strictly a concept) tends to be imagined as a thing.

This continuous reification of fishing possibilities partly explains why still today a fishing vessel borders between a secular and sacred place, where taboos should be observed. The two main verbal taboos are "priest" and "witch," considered to be the two mediators (sacred and profane) in Spanish culture between normal and abnormal reality. The (by definition) irregular or 'abnormal' effects of luck as a shift from the secular to the sacred are tabooed as well; for example, particularly during the dragging, no mention should be made of previous lucky voyages. A *pesca* was recently heard saying that he did not even like to be wished "good luck," but instead preferred "shit on luck."

The irregularity of the supply of fish that typifies this resource industry tends to make the fishermen reduce their perception of all events to only one causal framework, the natural order. They neglect social causation; that is, they tend to apply, fatalistically, natural laws to social realities. Just as luck corrects nature's irregularity but nature in itself remains arbitrary, so society tends to be seen as a reality independent of men's purposive action. This is partly why matters related to social or political organization are, to a great extent, absent from a fisherman's world view.

Besides the natural irregularity of fish, the constant danger at sea is another factor in creating a sense of fatalism in the fisherman's world view. At the end of our voyage, as winter was approaching and mechanical failures occurred, the presence of danger became increasingly felt. On four or five occasions, potentially tragic accidents occurred, as on 27 November, when the catch was so enormous (as much as fifty tons) that the stopper broke and the whole trawl slid back into the sea. "It was a miracle that it didn't kill four or five fishermen on deck," commented the *pesca*. Being pulled into Terranova waters would have meant death by exposure in just a couple of minutes. This almost happened when, on another occasion, the stopper broke and the net dragged a fisherman along the deck to the very edge of the ramp. The experience of risk could become as frightening as on 19 October, when the companion trawler was dangerously damaged by a storm and for three long hours the crew were afraid they would sink.

What originally is a psychological device to stave off fear, in the end prevents the search for, and eradication of, possible causes of danger. For example, seven crew members on our trawler had experienced a fire that sank the ship off the coast of St. Pierre during the previous voyage—a dreadful event which they used to relate vividly. This prompted me to ask a few fishermen whether they had seen a fire extinguisher on board, only to learn that they had neither seen nor looked for one. Since the fire had started in the galley, I asked our cook (who had been so shaken by the last galley fire that he never regained a feeling of security) if he had seen one. "You are right, we have no fire extinguisher in the galley, and I did not even realize it." As it was explained to me later, if there were to be a fire which would burn the entire trawler, it would happen despite any safety guarantee; and if there were to be no fire, then a fire extinguisher was useless.

Another occupational hazard is the absence of proper medical assistance at sea. In spite of the dangers involved, there is no doctor or medical assistant on board the whole Spanish fleet in Terranova. Each time a major accident occurs, the trawler has to make haste to St. John's or St. Pierre, each of which has a centre staffed by a Spanish doctor, a medical assistant and a social worker. There is also a Spanish priest in each of the ports.

A medical study of the effects that the work in a *pareja* has on the health of the fishermen could be revealing. From what I have heard, hardly anyone reaches the age of retirement. Fishermen frequently think of working in Terranova for a number of years and then changing to coastal or merchant ships at home. Another solution is to take jobs as oilers when the work on deck gets too heavy for older men. The cold is a major element contributing to the harshness of life at sea. One traditional remedy is to drink scalding hot coffee with cognac; on our trawler the average amount of coffee (mostly with cognac) drunk per day, per crew member, was nearly a litre. (Yet, except for the days in harbour, there was hardly a case of drunkenness aboard.)

Physical fatigue could become torture (some fishermen confessed to me at the end of the voyage that they never did properly recover from those November days of exhaustion). But of greater torture still is the dependence on the uncertainty of luck. The fishermen were happy that they were offered the opportunity of contributing with their fatigue to the all-powerful action of luck. Nobody would try to hide his extreme fatigue, but at the same time, those were the occasions at which fishermen's songs could be heard all over the mess hall and park.

When a Terranova fisherman states with renewed conviction, "This is not life," he means fishermen have no safety guarantees, no medical protection at sea, no trade unions, no family, no sex, no social life, no regular hours, no settled salary. Since he knows that any settled salary offered by the shipowner will be substantially lower than the salary he can get from sharing a percentage of the total profits, he prefers the shares, for that is the best payment system available. As a consequence, a fisherman's battle at sea becomes a battle not with the unsafe conditions, but with the uncertainty of luck and its arbitrary causation at the natural and social levels—a battle so long and arduous that he easily forgets how he came to struggle with unknown realities.

Disorder: A Sign of Luck

As pointed out above, the sense of disorder in the lives of fishermen stemmed from the nature of the working contract itself. First, the percentage of the gross profits that the fishermen were to receive was based on the shipowner's word. These profits, however, were ultimately governed by the uncertainty of the catches. Second, since the crew could not control the private sale of the fish by the shipowner, there was no way of accurately knowing what the real profits would be. Finally, the crew did not have a regular work schedule.

The work schedule is the best example of this irregularity. The total number of working hours on our trawler during the 126 days at sea (not counting the 16 days spent in port) was 1,041, which gives an average of 8 hours and 20 minutes per day. No fisherman on our trawler would admit that the above average was right; the overall feeling was that the working day lasted from 12 to 16 hours. The reason for this was that during the many hours when fishermen were not actually working, they experienced them not as time off but as periods of waiting. At the same time, I worked about 12 hours every day but was considered the one, by far, who (along with the cook) had more time to rest. Likewise, nobody on board questioned that the fishermen's schedule was heavier than the engineers' and oilers' schedule of 12 hours every day (except perhaps on Sundays, when they worked 10 hours).

The following sample of two consecutive days illustrates the disorder in the fishermen's work schedules. It shows essentially that the schedule for hauling and processing three tons of fish might allow the same time of rest as the schedule for hauling seventeen tons.

October 11-12 (three tons of net fish stored)

5:30 P.M.	fishermen are called for supper
6:00 P.M.	supper
6:30 P.M.	fishermen are ready to be called to haul in the net
7:30 P.M.	they are still waiting to be called
10:00 P.M.	fishermen are called to haul in the net
11:00 P.M.	fishermen start processing the fish; four fishermen remain on deck to repair the net
5:15 A.M.	fishermen finish processing the fish, change their working clothes and wash their hands
5:30 A.M.	breakfast

5:45 A.M. some fishermen go to bed; others prefer to stay up waiting to be called to haul in the companion trawler's net
7:00 A.M. fishermen are called to haul the net in
7:30 A.M. fishermen wait to cast their own net
9:00 A.M. fishermen are called to cast
10:00 A.M. fishermen wait for lunch
10:30 A.M. lunch
11:00 A.M. fishermen go to bed
3:30 P.M. fishermen are called to haul in their net

October 12–13 (seventeen tons of net fish stored)

3:30 P.M. fishermen are called to haul their own net back
5:00 P.M. fishermen cast the companion trawler's net
5:30 P.M. fishermen begin processing the fish
7:00 P.M. supper
4:00 A.M. breakfast
8:30 A.M. fishermen haul in the companion trawler's net
9:15 A.M. fishermen cast their own net
9:45 A.M. lunch
10:00 A.M. fishermen go to bed
3:30 P.M. fishermen are called to haul in their own net

In the 24 hours of the second schedule, the fishermen worked 18 hours to put away 17 tons of fish, with interruptions of only half an hour both for supper and breakfast and 5½ hours for sleep. In the 22 hours of the first schedule, the fishermen worked 8 hours to put away 3 tons and repair the net, but spent two intervals totalling 8 hours waiting to be called; the time left for sleep was 4½ hours. Psychologically, the 8 hours of work are certainly preferred to the 8 hours of waiting, for work offers its own economic reward, and waiting is felt to be an irritating waste of time which is neither work nor rest (when physical fatigue takes hold, only hours of sleep count as rest). Dragging day and night means that no time can be considered a safe time to rest, for the work can start again at any moment. Time of dragging and time of resting are conceptually opposed. This is made evident by the fact that the verbal taboos are observed particularly during the dragging.

Bou fishermen, with their two watches of six hours work and six hours rest, are much envied by the *pareja* fishermen. In a *pareja* only lunch and supper have an unchanging timetable. This schedule greatly helped to order the fishermen's social time on board when they were working during the day, but it disturbed their rest time when, after having worked the whole night, they were left with a half-dozen hours of sleep which necessarily had to be interrupted by lunch or supper. Frequently, this schedule forced them to waste part of their precious resting time waiting for the meals. The alternative was to not wake up to eat. (Eating heavily after long hours of work and immediately going to sleep was partly responsible for the many stomach problems.)

To sum up, even though the fishermen worked an average of eight or nine hours a day, they felt as though they worked sixteen, because the scattered hours of neither work nor rest could not be counted as free time. Furthermore, this irregularity itself became a symbol of efficiency and luck; the more fish came, the more irregular the work schedule became. However, if the catch was small, the *pesca* liked to call on the fishermen at any time, in part to make sure that they were constantly disposed to work. The underlying assumption behind this might be explained by the omnipotence and arbitrariness of luck; in case luck, subjected to regularity, lost its intrinsic power, the fishing schedule had to be set up from hour to hour according to the intuition of the *pesca*. Thus, the conceptual order based on luck partially justified disorder—at times even actually demanding it.

Notes

1. "The perception of the structural congruence between one set of processes, activities, relations, entities, and so on, and another set for which it acts as a program, so that the program can be taken as a representation, or conception—a symbol—of the programmed, is the essence of human thought" (Geertz 1973: 94).

2. Even in the absence of magical rites, although such rites had been used within memory.

3. The general stereotype of a *pesca* among the seamen describes him as being "one more fisherman without any education" who has been

chosen by a shipowner for his special qualities of experience at sea, knowledge of nets, and efficiency—or for being related to the shipowner. "He at any moment may be a fisherman again"; as an instance of this possibility the helmsman in the second trawler had once been a second *pesca*. In fact, the shipowner generally chooses first *pescas* from among second *pescas*, who in turn are appointed by first *pescas* from among family members.

In recent years, first *pescas* have been compelled to take a nine-month course for the title of "Patron of Deep-Sea Fishing." *Pesca* and "Patron of Deep-Sea Fishing" are therefore two categories that have recently been united in the same man.

CHAPTER 4

"*Terranova Is a Very Round Wheel*"

Whenever I remarked to the *pesca* about the catches we were having, he would retort, "Don't forget that Terranova is a very round wheel." For the Terranova fishermen, "round" is a metaphor of profound cognitive significance and the key to its meaning lies in the fishermen's perception of motion and space.

El balance, or "rolling" of the sea, refers to the lack of stability in fishermen's terrain, and Terranova waters, in particular, are known for their unbalanced nature; only in December did we have twelve days of total or partial lying to.

The words that indicate direction on land are different from those used at sea. At sea there is no left, right, ahead and behind. A fisherman does not say "The beer is in the front part of the cabin," but rather "The beer is in the bow part of the cabin"; and he does not say, "The rope is ahead of you," but "The rope is at bow," and so on, regardless of his individual position. Looking out from the deck of a ship, all one can see towards any direction is the circle of the horizon; no movement in any direction takes a ship closer to the horizon. The sense of motion in this spatial situation expresses a contradiction. In relation to the horizon, the ship never advances and is therefore immobile in the middle of the ocean; in relation to itself, however, it is in ceaseless but non-directional motion. At the basis of this contradiction is the absence of any stable exterior point of reference. No one, apart from the officer and the helmsman on the bridge, ever knows where north, south, east or west is, or in which directions Spain and Newfoundland lie. The four sides of the moving ship provide the only frame of orientation.

In its natural habitat, the fish are "down" in the water. Hauling the net in implies that fish come up from below. One verb, *virar*, is used for both "hauling the net in" and "taking it up"; conceptually, both operations involve the same movement. "Down" means "under the water"; "up" means "over the water," with the flat surface of the sea being the dividing plane. A word I never heard on the whole voyage was "sky," and when I asked about it, the reply was, "Our thoughts are always under the water." The sky/earth dichotomy on land becomes transformed into over-the-water/under-the-water. As to his own position, the fisherman is extremely aware of the fragility of his stability on the dividing line: horizontally, his space is reduced to a point in the middle of the sea; vertically, his space is an uncertain plane which does not stand still.

Anybody acquainted with fishermen's lives knows about their complaints about the lack of space on board. One captain referred to this problem as a claustrophobic illness that he named *mamparitis*, "the illness of the walls." Fishermen's referring to shipboard life as a prison points to this spatial constraint, among other things. "This is even worse than a prison," I was told, "because there you at least have stable ground." On our trawler the fishermen were sensitive to any fault in the spatial arrangement of the various parts of the ship, to the point that it was by far the main topic of conversation during the first days of sailing. Among fishermen and officers alike, endless complaints could be heard about the location of the galley, the clear run of the main deck, the lack of protection for the winch, the distribution of the park area, the misuse of space in the mess hall, the improper dimensions of the hold (too long and too low), the lack of communication between the lower deck and the galley, between the bridge and the galley, and so on. In the middle of the sea, surrounded by the immensity of space, which itself becomes contained inside the complete circle of the marine horizon, the seamen feel that the shortage of space on board can become unbearable.

The seaman's dominant visual image is a circle: round is the horizon that imprisons him, round are all the portholes through which the sight of the sea enters the ship, round is the steering wheel that traces the course, round is the fish finder through which the fish are found. The fishermen themselves sometimes discourse on this view of the world: "It is amazing how everything in this world is round. Take, for example, the ship. It can't move without a propeller that goes round and the steering wheel that goes round as well. Cars need wheels that are round. It is the same with airplanes; they need round wheels. Dishes, bottles, everything is round."

"Is the table round?" responded a fisherman during one such discussion, pointing to a square table.

"The screws that hold it are round."

"Is the design of your pants round?" argued the persistent fisherman, pointing to the showy squares of his pants.

"But the bottoms of your pants are round. Everything is round. Ships, cars, airplanes, nothing could be moved without wheels."

"When you walk, do you need wheels as well?" persisted the fisherman.

"Yes, walking too is going round, because the world itself moves in circles, and walking is going around."

"Are you round too?"

(Looking at his body and laughing) "No, I am not."

Significantly enough, the metaphor of "round" governed our working contracts as well, for the third clause stated: "The employee is classified, for all purposes, as *temporary* personnel of the enterprise, and the duration of the present voyage will be that *of a round voyage*." A round voyage means that it has no settled limit, that its completion depends on the shipowner's decision. The metaphor also appears in the songs the fishermen sang, such as this one:

> A stone in the road
> taught me that my destiny
> was to roll and roll
> to roll and roll

> Also a muleteer told me
> that there is no need of arriving first,
> but there is a need of arriving.
>
> (CHORUS)
> With money and without money
> I always do what I want
> and my word is law.
> I have no kingdom or throne
> or anybody who understands me,
> but I continue being king.
>
> And another stone in the road
> taught me that my destiny
> was to roll and roll,
> to roll and roll . . .[1]

To a fisherman, metaphorically, the visual image of the marine circle becomes the inner image of his own life: conceptually, a better living is unreachable; emotionally, he is alienated from family life by a distance of 2,000 miles and projective images. Being so distant from everything he misses, the fisherman ends up with the feeling that his desires constantly expressed in songs and private thoughts never reach fulfillment, just as a ship never reaches the horizon. Does his passion really have a direction? Is he not constantly betrayed by the torment of his own desire for stable land, family affection and a decent occupation which would not be defined as "this is not life"? He is a rolling stone; he feels nobody really knows about his inner exile; he sings: "I am going, I am going, to console my heart/ I am going, to banish this thought."

The economic product itself is not free from the metaphor for, as a fisherman ingeniously defined it, "the money of a fisherman is round; the money of a farmer is square." A farmer can grab his money, but not so a fisherman, whose money will soon go to his family's maintenance or else will be quickly spent—"This is a different money, for you earn it with so much suffering, but then also you spend it more easily, you don't look after it." It was also said, "Money means to be free from prison."

A number used in conversation countless times every day was

"four." In fact, it replaced the adverbs "several" and "a few"; whereas non-seamen usually say "several" people or "a few" things to indicate a small amount, the fishermen would say "four fish," "four people," "four things," "four days," and so on. As I was wondering what could be the reason for the persistent use of "four" among seamen, an imaginative correlation took form: environmentally, round horizon versus four parts of the ship; in spatial motion, unoriented immobility or non-directional full movement versus the directional motion of the ship with the four orientation poles attached to it; geometrically, circumference versus four-sided square; numerically, zero or everything (as round) versus four. Thus "four" and "square" stand for imaginary concreteness (as does the farmer's money) in a visual environment dominated by the indeterminateness of the round horizon.

Regarding the sense of time, a contradiction exists in connection with spatial motion. On the one hand, there is little temporal sequence on board ship; on the other hand, it appears as if time might not reach an end. Thus, it is not uncommon to hear among the fishermen, after three or four months at sea, expressions such as "I talked to him last week" or "I saw him the other day," referring by "last week" and "the other day" to the time prior to sailing, as if the months at sea did not count. Furthermore, we never felt sure when the voyage was going to end until three days before leaving for Spain. This was certainly a major worry throughout the whole voyage, particularly during the month of December. As a fisherman put it (on 22 December): "What kills me is to be thinking that you are going home one day and then to have to change it; first we were leaving on the 13th, then on the 20th, now on the 27th, and perhaps even on the 31st, or maybe later." The night we set course for Spain, several fishermen remarked how disturbing it was "when you have the idea of finishing up the voyage at a certain date and then that date is delayed." One fisherman made the significant remark that "it is yourself who creates this idea, since you are not told by the officers."

Not only does time seem to stop from the moment of departure, but the spatial reference previous to the voyage is taken on board. This was made clear to me on several occasions in St. John's harbour when, to my question of where they were from, fishermen replied, pointing to the ship, "I was born here," meaning "I was born in the same town where this ship belongs." It is as if the sea could not lay claim to a person, so that saying "here" or "now" when on board referred to the "here" and "now" previous to the sea voyage. "This is no life," the standard definition of life on board, had extended its meaning to "this is no time" and "this is no space."

At sea too, however, certain times and places are more real than others because they are filled with the symbols that bridge sea and land. Fish, money, work, economic luck—these are the main symbols that establish the connection with shore. The ocean crossing to and from Terranova, and the short distances covered on the banks, are a useless space for fishing. By contrast, "the bank," any bank, is a concrete place to inspect and mentally extend the boundaries of the ship's space. Below the bank's water is solid ground again, and the fishermen's attention becomes centred upon the space between the bottom and the surface. That space becomes an important mental domain of the fishermen.

The division between time on shore and time at sea, and the passage from one to the other, with all the emotional burden it bears, are mentally realized through dates that are invested with enormous significance. Undesired changes in those 'liminal' dates can create considerable personal and social disturbances. The fishermen use the expressive saying *hacer firme*, "to make it firm," on two occasions: when they return to port and moor the ship to the wharf; and when the net is shot away and the trawl is fixed by the stopper at the stern side, leaving loose on deck the cable that ties it to the winch. Thus, when the trawl is dragging on the bottom of the marine soil, the trawler is "firm," and the very round wheel of Terranova fishing is made steady for once.

Just as the spatial nullity of the ship is brought about by the immensity of the sea, likewise, metaphorically, the catches of fish never satisfy the logical and affective expectations of fishing. Just as no linear space can be visualized outside the ship's contour, likewise no linear thinking can lead to luck. The marine horizon lays down the visual boundaries beyond which no space can be imagined, and luck establishes the mental boundaries beyond which no event can be predicted.

If "last week" can mean "the week before we left home port three months ago," if (as I was told by the *pesca*) "mathematics do not apply at sea," and if "luck" means "arbitrary causation," then we are close to admitting that being at sea creates a cultural environment in which we are free from the usual spatial, temporal and quantitative notions that serve as anchors for our causal thinking. The loosening of causal thinking that results makes it possible to fix on a random circumstance as the cause of an event. An illustration of this is my visit to a trawler in St. John's harbour, during which something got broken on board; the *pesca* of the trawler associated my presence with bad luck and did not want me on board again.

In a world view constructed around the keystone of luck, the most powerful cause is the possible absence of a cause; the most feared luck is "no luck," and strong emotions are attached to non-events. With the negation of linear causation resulting from the arbitrariness of luck, the sense of order is disturbed, since order in Western culture is, by definition, linear (Lee 1958). If the absence of causation (luck) is a constant threat, then the definition of the objective anchors (temporal, spatial, quantitative, causal, and so on) for evaluating events becomes a matter of the mood of the moment, as determined by a recent catch, or other factors. For example, what made a week of 120 tons such a magnificent week was, first, the uncertainty that it could happen and, second, the fact that the average weekly yield was but 40 to 50 tons.

"Whatever must be, will be" summarizes the fishermen's philosophy when danger or a major accident occurs. The extent of danger involved in fishing in the Spanish *parejas* has been acknowledged by people who have fished in other fleets in the North Atlantic (W. Warner, personal communication). Situations that later were recognized as potentially fatal occurred several times during our voyage. The usual risks associated with fishing are increased considerably in a *pareja* because of the enormous dimensions and weight of the trawl (seven tons) together with the volume of the haul, which could easily be forty to sixty tons. This amount has to be taken in with the help of bridles, stoppers, ropes, blocks, tackles, and other equipment which is never quite safe when handling such weights. In the particularly unlucky months of March to July of 1977, in an industry employing less than 2,000 workers, the following accidents took place: five fishermen died in fires; two men died by falling into the water; a fishermen died when he fell down a gangway and broke his neck; a chief engineer lost his leg when it was cut off by a stopper. In order not to be paralyzed by the fear of an accident, it is necessary to create a belief in which everything is regulated by fate and according to which "nothing happens until your day comes." Furthermore, "when your day comes, there is nothing you can do to prevent it." Note should be made again of the fishermen's lack of political, economic and legal rights. There appears to be a close connection between such deprivations and the fatalistic ideology of the fishermen.

"Terranova is a vice" expresses the fishermen's sentiments about fishing in Newfoundland waters. The expression refers to their playing with 'chancy' money; to their awareness of tricking themselves with the thought of saving most of their earnings; to their disdain of letting themselves surrender to economic constraints, as well as to the suffering and arbitrariness that Terranova fishing represents; to the pleasure taken in the vicious circle of gambling with luck. I was repeatedly told that fishermen who had once fished in Terranova tend to return after sailing for a while in merchant ships, or after doing some coastal fishing. It was not because of greed for money or the lack of adaptation to shore life, but simply for the luxury of "vice," that they would return to Terranova. Fishing is, then, a kind of play. Like black clubmen in Bermuda, the Terranova fishermen follow their pursuit "for its own sake, its own rewards, its own emotional satisfactions"—and there is an "important relationship between play and thought" (Manning 1973: xv).

Fishing, like hunting, creates its own psychology: hours and days of expectant watch in order to enjoy, in the end, the instant reward for the long wait. The expectation in itself becomes part of the game, a constant wager with the natural environment. Each time a fisherman goes on deck to haul in the net, he experiences the thrill of facing the enigmatic working of luck, which, at any time, can be portentous. A fisherman who, day after day, year after year, becomes accustomed to gambling with luck is unlikely to adapt happily to shore life in the event he is compelled to abandon the sea because of illness, retirement or family pressures.

The gambler's psychology is part of the fishermen's ethos. Gambling with luck takes hold of the fishermen's psyche and is partially responsible for their lack of interest in other matters. On our trawler, there were four radios, but it was a rare occasion if a fisherman used his free time to listen to the news, despite the important political and social events going on in Spain at the time. (Sunday afternoon football results, however, were listened to.) No matter how eagerly a fisherman wants to return home, once he is there, "the sea pulls him back" after two or three weeks. Where does a fisherman actually live? His most real experience is always somewhere in the distance. When at sea, his desire is fixed on shore; when on shore, he is afraid that his stay there, away from his job, might be too long.

Deprivation is the fisherman's way of creating accomplishment. Postponed earnings become compulsory savings since no one is paid until the end of the voyage. The fisherman regards this aspect of his work as a bonus. In contrast to his life at sea—where no real leisure is possible for months, where his mind is constantly straining to reach the source of luck—nothing but rest is available to him during the twenty to thirty days at home, and his mind lies fallow. At sea the emotional gratification of the family is felt as an absence, but once at home, nothing but family life takes up his time. From nothing to everything and vice versa (to the point that both poles tend to be confused)—this is the occupational pattern of deep-sea fishing.

This polarity is not only between sea and shore. At each pole, too, there is a polarity between the experience of actual reality (social and ecological relations) and the experience of imaginative reality (dependence on luck, emotional projection to shore). For example, although the situation at sea is regarded as one of emotional deprivation of the family, at the same time the fantasy experience of it is so keen that the emotional gratification derived from it can become a kind of vice as well. My suspicions about this were confirmed when a particularly intelligent fisherman confessed to me that he was going to sea partly so that he would not lose the emotional intensity that distance from family creates. The confinement at sea becomes an emotional investment for deep-sea fishermen. "You are good when you are gone," conclude some. From the feeling that he is loved *because* he is away fulfilling his duty, the fisherman might end up wondering whether he is not better off staying away and unconsciously preferring the emotional enjoyment of fantasy experience.

The same tendency to confuse actual and imaginary reality can turn into psychological distortions. For example, the cook prefers the winter voyage (which, in Terranova, is particularly cruel) to the summer voyage, because in winter "you know that the weather will go on improving, while in summer you have to expect that it will get worse." Similarly, the *pesca* mentioned a fisherman who used to enjoy a day of bad weather because "tomorrow will be better." In both cases, the actual event becomes secondary: bad weather with good expectations is preferable to good weather with bad expectations; imaginary reality is treated as the more significant.

In any case, both the actual order and the imagined one tend to be experienced simultaneously, because of "life at a distance." Conditions at sea tend to obliterate the boundaries between order and disorder, for actual disorder can be validated as a possible cause of order. On one occasion, a drunken fisherman was awake when a fire broke out and so he was able to sound the alarm. This event was given the following interpretation: "You see, at sea everything is different. You can never say that something is wrong. Even drunkenness can be all right; if he had not got drunk, several fishermen would have died in the fire." Furthermore, certain kinds of disorders may become symbols of order. Luck being, by definition, an uncontrollable cause, its actualization is accompanied by disordered schedules and periods of heavy work that in themselves reflect luck. Since luck is the key ordering concept, the order that matters is the arbitrary causation—any other concept of order is only a substitute.

Consequently, the fisherman is confronted with psychological contradictions in his perception of his work and status as fisherman. On the one hand, he complains about the shipowner's exploitation and the *pesca*'s high salary; on the other hand, he is 'lucky' when he is punished by long hours of work, and he can accept a *pesca* who forces him to join his unrelenting pursuit of fish. Likewise, the fisherman feels humiliated in his occupation, which he regards as "the lowest work," but at the same time he is proud of "being a fisherman"; he would like to have more dignified work, but he cannot give up being a fisherman; as a crew member, he depends on every other member, but he is constantly self-assertive; he sings, "What a little slave life, the life of a fisherman," but he reacts against anyone who becomes embittered on board.

A Terranova fisherman once made this comparison: "A fisherman is like a good-time girl who wastes her life quickly but enjoys it intensely. A farmer is like a servant maid who arranges her life in an orderly way but, after all, is a servant who does not enjoy it."

"Once means forever" was the argument the cook used to stop me from doing things that I was not obliged to do as cookee. As noted previously, custom on board is basically regulated by the principle that "what you do once becomes law." Once you have a point, all you have to do to form a circle is to turn it around; once a new social fact has been granted, all you have to do to make it law is to repeat it again. By such means, generalizations are established in the social order. Luck has a similar mission in the ideological order. It places the actual fishing within a more general order, in relation to which the catches become signs. Under the assumption of luck, what actually occurs is secondary to what may have occurred or to what may occur. Conceptually, the emphasis at sea is in having luck rather than in having a good catch.

"We think only of fish and family." Both kinds of generalization (luck and family) are connected with the sea/shore dichotomy. Both spheres of reality are felt by the fishermen as simultaneous and at the same time incompatible. Both are totalities that tend to exclude each other in the fishermen's experience; both are wholes that are made into parts opposing each other, and into parts that resist being defined as such, lest they lose their nature of being generalizations, classes, logico-emotional devices. Thus the familiar contradictions emerge: luck rules the world, but its place is the sea; the goal of life is family love, but it remains on shore. Where there is luck, no enjoyment of love is possible; where there is family, the uncertainty of luck should not be permitted. At sea, shore and family life can only be experienced through projections; on shore, sea and luck are experienced through the difficulty a fisherman has in adapting to shore life.[2]

The fisherman's view of the economic and natural orders is conditioned by luck. The gaps in the commonsense view of the world are covered by the cognitive system created by luck; that is, luck and its permutations guide the fisherman's thinking which corrects the daily fluctuations of fish. The principle of luck among fishermen is a solution to the central cognitive problem of how nature works: all the economic anxiety becomes focused on the intellectual problem of how natural causation can be understood and patterned. Luck governs events, relations and classifications. Possibilities are as conceptually real as actualities. The primary causation of events is arbitrary but self-correcting; man is directly dependent on nature for his survival.

We have seen how fishermen tend to be caught in contradictory and ambivalent behaviour, such as responsibility and irresponsibility towards luck, fidelity and infidelity towards wife, rebellion against and identification with the *pesca*, contempt and pride in being fishermen, and so on. These patterns of behaviour are learned by the fishermen and constitute the cultural expression of fishing. The Terranova fishermen's situation can be summed up in their own view of their occupation—"This is not life." Terranova is "a vice," a vicious circle of self-denial and economic reward of self-contempt and love for the family.

Contradiction and ambivalence are found in the fishermen's reactions to the declaration by Canada of the 200-mile limit. On the one hand, they are aware that the new regulations may mean for them the sudden loss of their jobs and their "Terranova" wages; on the other hand, as one fisherman said, "Let them [shipowners, *pescas*] come here now." One *pesca* recognized, "At least now we won't kill ourselves here." The last turn of the Terranova wheel seems to be unavoidably approaching its end; despite the extent of their knowledge that "everything is luck," the Spanish Terranova fishermen still needed one more lesson: luck is not only a device to help men allure fish; luck can also decide that fish remain even while men vanish.

Definitely, Terranova was a very round wheel.

Notes

1. This song was popular in Spain about a quarter century ago; among the fishermen it remains current.

2. Such a state of affairs probably helps explain why high rates of psychoses, particularly schizophrenia, have been noted among fishermen (Aubert 1965: 243). Although statistics about Spanish seamen are not available, any Terranova officer or fisherman would bear witness to the high number of mental derangements among his mates.

APPENDIX

Fluctuations of Catches

The graphs on the following pages that represent catches by day are based on data from my own voyage. The other graphs, showing variations per month over a period of years, are drawn from the experience of a crew member who had fished on a number of trawlers.

Daily fluctuations of our trawler's catches during the month of September

Daily fluctuations of our trawler's catches during the month of October

Daily fluctuations of our trawler's catches during the month of November

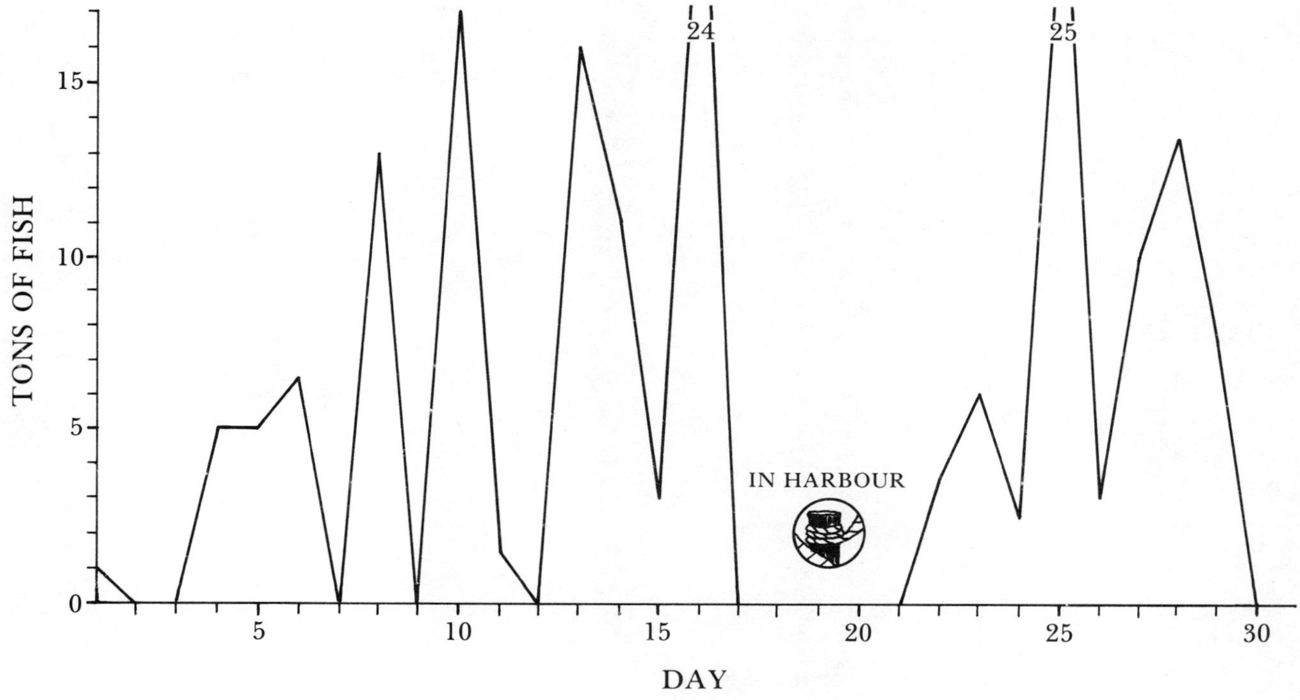

Daily fluctuations of our trawler's catches during the month of December

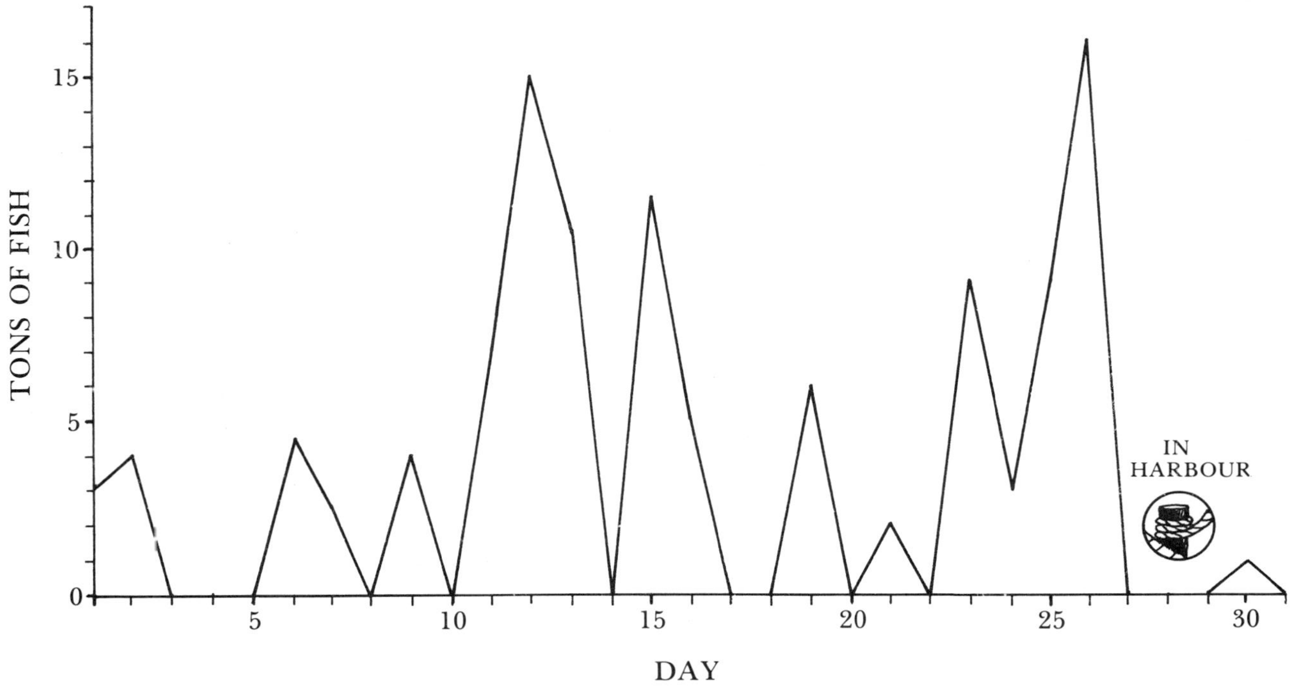

Total and monthly fluctuations of consecutive voyages (one trawler)

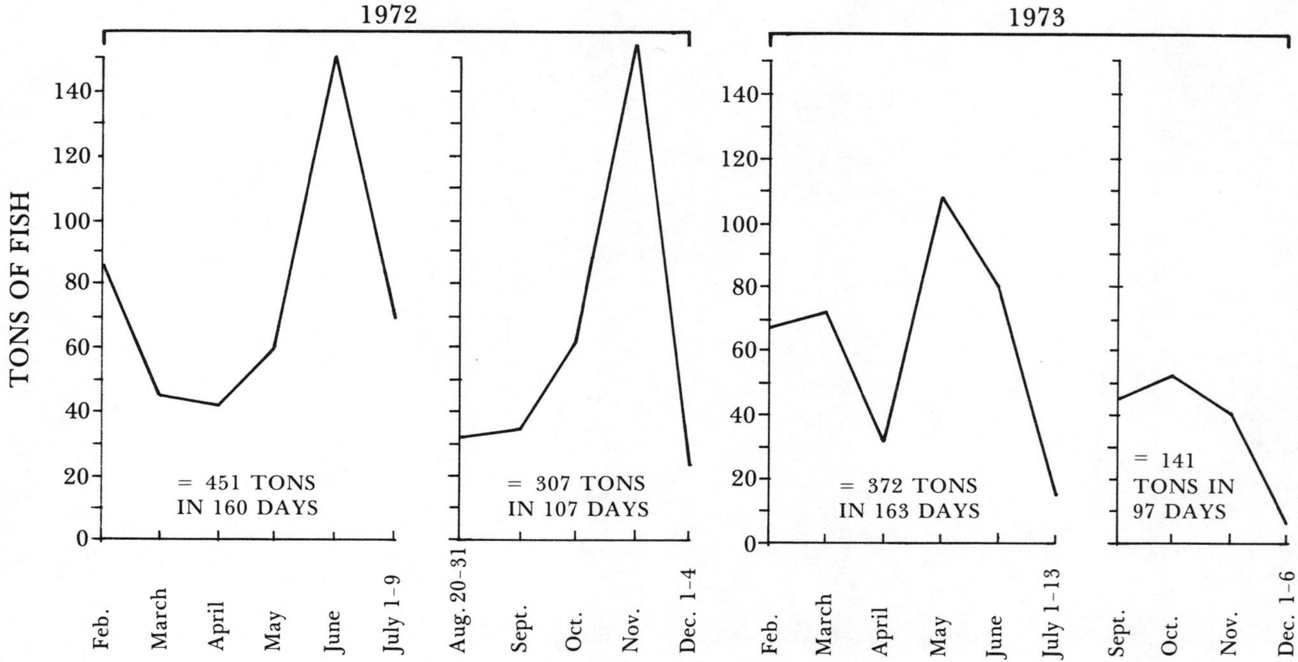

Total and monthly fluctuations of consecutive voyages (*continued*)

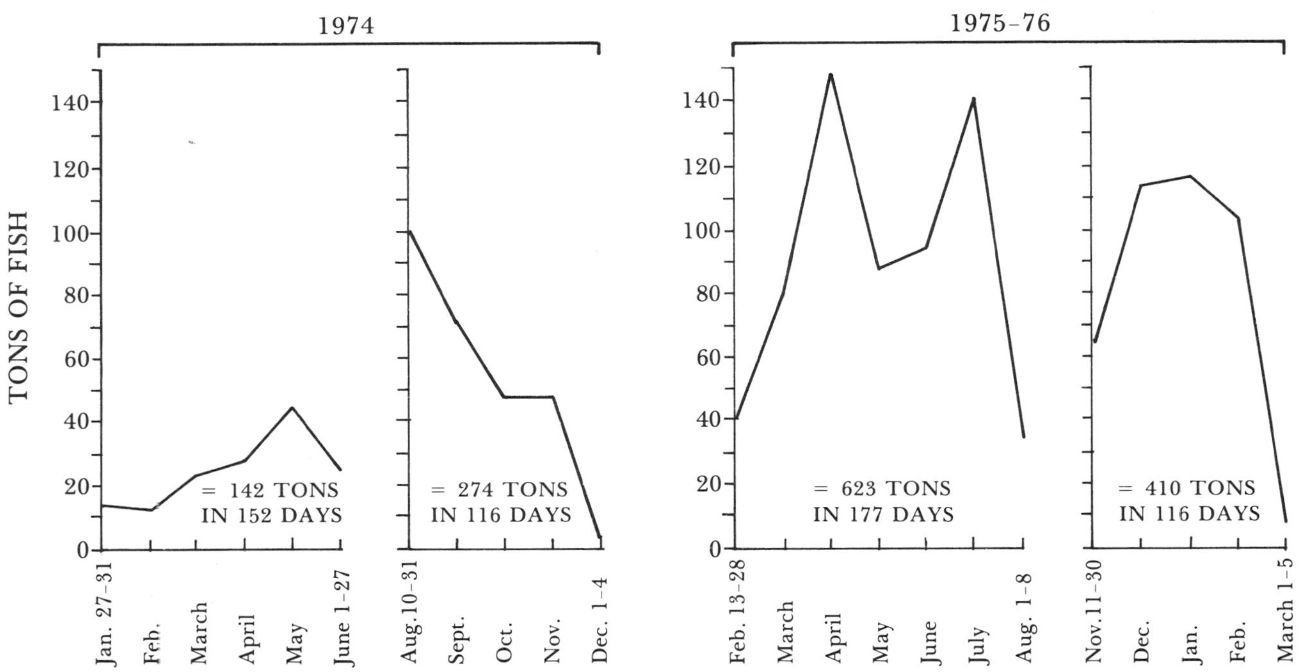

References

Andersen, Raoul, and Cato Wadel
    1972   Comparative Problems in Fishing Adaptations. In R. Andersen and C. Wadel, eds., *North Atlantic Fishermen: Anthropological Essays on Modern Fishing*. St. John's: Institute of Social and Economic Research, Memorial University of Newfoundland.

Aubert, Vilhelm
    1965   A Total Institution: The Ship. In V. Aubert, ed., *The Hidden Society*. Totowa, N.J.: Bedminster Press.

Barth, Fredrik
    1966   *Models of Social Organization*. Royal Anthropological Institute Occasional Paper no. 23. London.

Bateson, Gregory
    1936   *Naven: A Survey of the Problems Suggested by a Composite Picture of the Culture of a New Guinea Tribe Drawn from Three Points of View*. Cambridge: Cambridge University Press.
    1972   *Steps to an Ecology of Mind*. San Francisco: Chandler.

D.I.S. (Departamento de Investigación de Sociologia)
    1972   *Estudio sociológico hombres de la mar*. Cuaderno informativo, no. 8, "La Familia del marino" (Régimen interno). Madrid.

Durkheim, Emile, and Marcel Mauss
    1963   *Primitive Classification*. Translated from the French and edited with an introduction by Rodney Needham. Chicago: University of Chicago Press.

Faris, James C.
    1968   Validation in Ethnographical Description: The Lexicon of "Occasions" in Cat Harbour. *Man* (n.s.) 3(1).

References

Fernandez, James W.
   1974   The Mission of Metaphor in Expressive Culture. *Current Anthropology* 15(2).

Geertz, Clifford
   1973   *The Interpretation of Cultures: Selected Essays by Clifford Geertz.* New York: Basic Books.

Leach, Edmund
   1976   *Culture and Communication: The Logic by Which Symbols are Connected. An Introduction to the Use of Structuralist Analysis in Social Anthropoligy.* Cambridge: Cambridge University Press.

Lee, Dorothy
   1958   Linear and Non-linear Codifications of Reality. In D. Lee, *Freedom and Culture.* Englewood Cliffs, N.J.: Prentice-Hall.

Manning, Frank
   1973   *Black Clubs in Bermuda: Ethnography of a Play World.* Ithaca, N.Y.: Cornell University Press.

Mariño, Antón L.
   1977   Pesqueria galega: a crisis dun sistema. *Teima* 7(27).

Ordenanza de Trabajo
   1976   Ordenanza de Trabajo para la pesca marítima en buques bacaladeros. *Boletín oficial del estado* (Madrid) 97.

Soroa, J. M. Ruiz
   1976a   La ley penal en la picota. *Hombres del mar* 122.
   1976b   Ley penal y disciplinaria. Proyecto de ponencia al Congreso del SLMM (Sindicato Libre de la Marina Mercante). Unpublished paper.

Schwimmer, Erik
   1973   *Exchange in the Social Structure of the Orokaiva.* New York: St. Martin's Press.

Tanner, Adrian
   1979   *Bringing Home Animals: Religious Ideology and Mode of Production of the Mistassini Cree Hunters.* Social and Economic Studies no. 23. St. John's: Institute of Social and Economic Research, Memorial University of Newfoundland.

Warner, William W.
   1977   The Politics of Fish. *The Atlantic* 240(2).

Wittgenstein, Ludwig
   1961   *Tractatus Logico-Philosophicus.* Translated by D. F. Pears and B. F. McGuinness. London: Routledge and Kegan Paul. Originally published in 1921.

Index

Andersen, Raoul, and Wadel, Cato, ix
Aubert, Vilhelm, x
Authority and role structure, 6-12, 20-29
Author's field work, xi-xii
   See also Cookee
Ayudantia de Marina, 15

Banquereau, xi
Bateson, Gregory, 45
Bou, x, 14
   versus *pareja*, 1, 4, 13, 92
Bridge, 16-17, 18

Captain, 7, 86
   authority of, 7, 11, 20-21
   versus *pesca*, 11-12, 20-24, 86
Cartilla, 15, 61
Comandancia de Marina, 15
Cook, xi, 21-22, 28
   role of, 47
Cookee, role and status of, xi-xii, 25, 28, 31
Costa, 11-12
Crew solidarity, 49-50, 70, 87
Custom, sovereignty of, 26-29

Daily schedule of fishermen, 91-92
Decision-making, 7, 23
Deck, 16-19
   diagram of upper and lower, 18-19

Ecology, mental, ix-x, 66, 95
   See also Psychodynamics *and* Luck

Economics of *pareja*, 4-6, 14
Emotional life of fishermen, 33-62
   collective control of emotions, 49-50
   distant reality of the family, 36-39
   fantasy of returning home, 34
   group versus individual loyalty, 51-56
   importance of cooking to, 48
   letters and songs, 39-40
   relations between fishermen, 45
   social deprivations, 35-36
   suppressing fear, 58
Ethos, definition of, 34

Fishermen
   and adaptation to shore, 40-42, 61, 106
   characteristics of, 60
   and custom as regulator of behaviour, 26-29
   and daily schedule, 91-92
   deprivations of, 13, 35-36, 43-45
   and disorder, 78, 90-91, 101, 104
   emotional life of, 33-62
   exploitation of, 14, 29, 84
   and the family, 33, 35, 36-39, 43-45, 59, 61, 103-104, 106
   and fatalism, 72, 76, 88, 101
   and fishing manoeuvres, 3-4
   and fish processing, 4
   and foreign ports, 39, 42
   and gambler's psychology, 41, 103
   and God, 59-60
   and health, 89-90, 93

Fishermen *(cont.)*
  and law, 12-16
  legal rights of, 13, 15
  and luck, 66-93, 100, 101, 102, 103, 104, 105, 106
  and mental illness, 55
  psychodynamics of, 34-35, 41-42, 43-44, 53, 56, 66, 70, 88-89, 90, 93, 98, 99-106
  psycholinguistics of, 95-99
  and risk, 88-89, 101-102
  and sex, 43-45
  self-concept of, 56-58, 60
  social organization of, x, 20-26
  status of, 29, 56-57, 60-61
  wages of, 5-6
Fishing as a cultural system, ix, x, xi, 106
  See also Fishermen *and* Luck
Fishing gear, 2
Fishing manoeuvres, 1-4, 23
  and boatswain, 3
  casting, 2
  and deckhands, 3
  dragging, 1, 23
  and engineer, 3
  hauling in, 2, 3-4
  and helmsman, 3
  letting out, 2, 3
  and *pesca*, 3
Fishing as ritual, 81-82
Fish processing, 4, 23
Foreign ports, 39, 42
Franco, 14

Galician labour, xi
Galley, 16-20, 21
  importance to social interaction, 47-48
Gambler's psychology of fishermen, 41, 103
Geertz, Clifford, ix, 87
Geographical location of voyage described, xi
God, role of, 59-60
Grand Banks, xi
Greenland, xi, 70

Health of fishermen, 89-90, 93
  mental, 55

Hold, 17-19

Law and Spanish fishing, 12-16
  Marine Military Jurisdiction, 12, 15
  Ordinance of Work, 13
  Penal and Disciplinary Law, 12
Lee, Dorothy, 101
Leisure activities, 20
Luck
  bad luck, 68; example of, 71, 72
  and crew solidarity, 87
  and the daily catch (its effects on fishermen's psyche, 77-81) (as regulator of fishermen's psyche, 87, 100-106)
  fishermen's conceptions of, 67-68, 75, 80
  formulaic aspect of, 87
  having luck, 87, 105, 79; example of, 68, 71, 74
  and the human order, 66-68, 75, 106
  and the natural order, 66, 88, 106
  no luck, 68; example of, 71
  and the *pesca*, 82-85, 86
  reification of, 81-82, 88
  relation to work, 66-67
  responsibility for, 76-77, 82-86

Manning, Frank, 102
Marine Military Jurisdiction, 12, 15
Mental illness among fishermen, 55

Northeast Atlantic, ix
Northwest Atlantic, ix

Order and disorder, 101, 104
Ordinance of Work, 13

Pareja
  authority structure of, 6-12, 20-29
  definition of, x, 1
  economics of, 4-6, 14
  legal and technological aspects of, 1-31
  recruitment to, 7-11
  in relation to *bou*, 1, 4, 13, 92
  spatial layout of, 16-20
  technology of, 1-4, 7, 23

Park, 16-19

Index

Pesca, 7, 69
  authority of, 11, 20-23
  definition of, 2
  first *pesca*, 7, 25
  mediator of luck, 82-87
  qualifications of, 85-86
  reputation of, 2
  second *pesca*, 7, 25
  versus captain, 11, 21-24, 86
Psychodynamics of fishermen
  absence of linear thinking, 99-102
  beliefs regarding fishing occupation, 66
  born to be a fisherman, 56
  effects of no horizon, 98
  effects of uncertainty, 90, 93
  fantasy, 103-104
  gambling psychology, 103
  land versus sea, 34-35, 41-43, 103-106
  private relations, 53, 55
  reduction of causal thinking to natural order, 88-89
  sexual ethics, 43-45

Quota imposition, xi
  fishermen's reaction to, 106-107

Recruitment, 7
Risk among fishermen, 72, 88-89, 101-102

St. John's, xi, 70, 71
St. Pierre, xi, 15, 70, 73
Salaries of officers, 6
Seamen's terminology, 81, 95-99
Self-concept of fishermen, 56-58, 60
Sexual mores, 43-45
Shipowner, xi, 4-5, 7, 14, 86-87
Ship's layout, 16-20

Social organization (structure), x, 20-26
  captain's authority, 20-23
  and cultural system, x
  fishermen, 25-26
  pesca's authority, 21-23
  petty officers, duties of, 24; relation to fishermen, 25
  and ship's layout, 17-20
Social relations on board, 21, 23, 25-30, 46-62, 70
  between fishermen and *pesca*, 82-85
Socio-cultural concomitants of fishing *See* Fishermen
Soroa, J. M. Ruiz, 15
Spanish fishing industry
  militarization of, 12-15
  in North Atlantic, xi
  in Terranova, x, 4-5
Status of fishermen, 29, 56-57, 60-61
Stella Maris club, 15

Technology of *pareja*, x, 1-4, 7, 23
Terranova, 1
  definition of, ix, 102
Terranova voyages, xi, 34
Trade unions, absence of, 14
Trawl
  composition of, 2
  importance to *pareja*, 2
  and *pesca*'s reputation, 2

Vigo, xi, 61

Wages of fishermen, 5-6
Warner, William W., xi
Wittgenstein, Ludwig, 65
Wives, 43, 44
  attitude to husband's occupation, 40

1 2 3 4 5 6 7 8 9 10 11 12 13   90 89 88 87 86 85 84 83 82 81